THE LAYMAN AND HIS CONSCIENCE

A RETREAT

by Ronald Knox

SHEED & WARD - NEW YORK

Contents

The Layman and His Conscience

I "He's Asking for You"

I THOUGHT, by way of introduction to our retreat, we would make an effort of the imagination; try to carry ourselves back across the centuries to a particular incident recorded in the gospels, recorded most poignantly by St. Mark. I mean the story of the blind man called Bartimaeus (Mark x, Luke xviii) who sat by the wayside begging, just when our Lord was passing, for the last time, through Jericho. "Hearing a multitude pass by"—that is St. Luke; he always has an eye for detail. Bartimaeus wasn't like you and me, couldn't see the crowds sweeping along the road; but he heard the tramping and the chatter, and asked what was up. So they told him that Jesus of Nazareth was going past; and all at once he changed his tune of "Pity the poor blind man" for something more definite, "Jesus, son of David, have pity on me." Ridiculous, of course, to suppose that he could be heard at a distance, with all the noise of the street around him, and the cries of the street vendors; but still he went on, in his monotonous beggar's voice, "Jesus, son of David, have pity on me." After a time, the people around him got annoyed, and told him to shut up: did he suppose he was the only person of any importance, that Jesus of Nazareth should stop and talk to the likes of him? But still he goes on; and then, in the middle of the road, our Lord turns round and says, "I want to have a word with that blind man." All at once he ceases to be regarded as a nuisance, and becomes a hero; the people round him are impressed, and St. Mark has preserved for us the very words they used to him; words which strike the ear, after all these centuries, with a kind of magic. *Animaequior esto; surge, vocat te*—"It's all right; come along; he's asking for you."

Our Lord, as we know, could have restored his sight without looking round, by a mere act of will. But he wouldn't do miracles like that. The blind man has sat all these years, a beggar unnoticed in a row of beggars, except when some charitable penny jingled in his cap. Now, he is to be made to feel important; he is singled out for a special interview. "Can I do anything for you?" "Yes, you can give me back my sight." And he looks up, and sees his own image in the eyes of Jesus Christ.

A single person, lost in a crowd, all those centuries ago; but pinpointed, as long as history lasts, by the fact that our Lord stopped and took notice of him. I want you to think of your retreat as a solitary interview which our Lord has seen fit to grant you. I want you to apply to yourself those words which were addressed to the blind man, words of reassurance, of exhortation, and of invitation; *Animaequior esto, surge, vocat te;* It's all right, come along; he's asking for you.

The times in which we live have, increasingly, the effect of depersonalizing us, of making each of us feel a mere unit in the population. Your dust-bin is just like everybody else's dust-bin; the milk-bottles at your door are indistinguishable from the milk-bottles next door; your chimneypots are just like everybody else's chimney-pots—"they don't make any other kind now, there's no demand for them." The number of your car, the number of your telephone, the number of your income-tax return, they all label you as a unit, not a person; not Mr. or Mrs. or Miss So-andso, but Number So-and-so. You are fifteenth on the list to have your windows cleaned, last but one in the bus queue. People come round and ask whether you want capital punishment abolished, whether you think it would be a good thing to fly to the moon, and your name goes down with several hundreds of thousands of people, a cross-section of the population. You will do as well as anybody else, anybody else will do as well as you. You are not a person any longer.

And then you come into retreat, and find that our Lord is asking for you. Not for anybody else, for you.

Animaequior esto—be calm, it's all right; yes, he asked for you personally, not for "the occupant of Room number So-and-so"; he calls his own sheep by name. He is interested in everything about you, even the things that bore other people, your health, your foibles, your scruples. He cares as much for you individually as if you were the only soul he had ever created; God doesn't do things— can't do things—by halves. He arranged to meet you here; arranged that you should go into retreat just now, with this particular background of worries and problems which you brought in with you. You, on your side, had almost given up the struggle to preserve your own identity; were prepared to treat yourself as just an average Christian, taking your cue from the rest, looking round to see what they did and falling into line with them. You would be one of a crowd, and sooner or later, please God, you would rush the barriers into heaven as one of a crowd, while nobody was looking. "You didn't really think that?" he says. "When a soul reaches its heaven, it is always a separate event; its course has been mapped out for it beforehand, and it achieves its destiny just so, and not anyhow else. We had a plan, hadn't we, for your life? And I have come to see how it is getting on. Not very brilliantly, I expect; never mind—*animaequior esto*, be calm about it." It *is* important, I think, to be calm about it when we go into retreat; to see ourselves just as we are, not some fancied projection of ourselves; to take stock of the actual situation which has got to be dealt with here and now, not to waste time over imaginary situations which (for better or worse) we might get into. Don't overstrain your mind, don't indulge in rhetoric; be calm.

You'd have expected our Lord, wouldn't you, to cross the road and go up to where the blind man sat, cross-legged, in the hedgerow. "I will come and heal him"—if our Lord was prepared to accompany the centurion on an errand of mercy like that, surely he wouldn't grudge crossing the street for the sake of a blind man? After all, it isn't very easy for blind people to get about; Bartimaeus can feel his way along the wall to find the exact place where he sits down daily to beg; but to go out among a crowd of people, groping his way and stumbling over the loose stones, in mere obedience to the sound of a voice—surely that was asking rather much of him? He can do it, of course; "Oh, wants me to come and speak to him, does he? All right, just hold my stick—give me a hand, neighbour, while I get to my feet, there's such a crowd everywhere—now, where did I put my cloak? Mustn't leave that behind; we blind people have to be careful about our property—take my hand, will you, and tell me where I'm putting my feet—not too fast, not too fast, easy does it."

That is the sort of picture you might form for yourself, if you read the story in St. Luke. Now turn to St. Mark; St. Mark was there, I take it; he knows the blind man by name, Bartimaeus, son of Timaeus; perhaps he was even offering to lend a helping hand. And he describes what happened. The blind man "threw away his cloak, and leapt to his feet, and so came to Jesus." Our Lord knew his man; if he summoned him, it was so as to give him the chance of doing just that—bestirring himself and making a venture of faith, as the condition of his healing.

Yes, "rise up"; our Lord demanded of the blind man something in the way of initiative; he demands the same of you. Not any sudden, not any heroic initiative; he knows his man. No, but he does expect you to do something in the way of preparation; if he is to speak to you, you must try to make a silence and a solitude in which his voice can make itself heard. Keep a silence, as far as possible, in your mind. At the same time, try to keep your mind, as far as possible, supple and elastic. Don't tie yourself up beforehand with resolves to perform such and such a devotion at such and such a time. If you are doing the Stations, and find they aren't going well, drop them. Keep your liberty of spirit, ready to spread your sails to any breath of divine inspiration that comes to you.

And then there is just that third point to be considered; our Lord is calling you. That, you object, sounds ridiculous; God's call comes to people like St. Francis and St. Joan of Arc, setting them apart from the rest of their generation to do some important, some sensational work for him. At least, that's not quite true, because we do talk about the clergy and the religious having a vocation, and a vocation must after all be the same kind of thing as a call. But I haven't to make up my mind about any major decision—one way and another, I'm quite satisfied that my present state of life is the state of life in which he means me to serve him. What should I need a call for? What would he be calling me away from, and what to?

Yes, I know; but I don't think that's the only kind of call our Lord has for us. After all, he didn't call Bartimaeus to be an apostle, or to any very special vocation as far as we know. He isn't venerated anywhere, I think, as a saint. No, all we hear is that when he got back his sight he followed Jesus on his way; and that, if you come to think of it, is something which is expected from all of us. The good Shepherd calls his own sheep by name, and leads them out; oughtn't we to think of him as running his eye over the flock, and giving a warning shout now here, now there, now to you, now to me, when he sees us beginning to stray out of our true course? And that, surely, is what a retreat is meant for.

We are not, please God, blind as Bartimaeus was, but our spectacles have got a good deal furred over, haven't they?

We don't see straight always; we mistake the things that aren't worth having, the things that aren't worth doing, for the things that are. And when he asks us what he can do for us, we still have to answer, "Lord, give me back my sight! Give me back the clear sight I had when I was fresh from school, with all the influences of a Catholic training; give me back the clear sight I had when I was a new convert, and my way was all mapped out for me in black and white. Give me back the power to see things straight, as they really are!"

If you take my advice (people very seldom do), you won't spend your time in retreat examining your present way of life through a magnifying glass and finding holes in it and making resolutions about how to mend them. Leave that alone for the present; if you can manage to finish the retreat with clearer eyes, those holes will be discovered, those resolutions will suggest themselves, easily enough, as you go along. Try to get as near our Lord as possible, open your heart to him as much as possible; unite your will to the will of God, and leave the rest to him.

2 Dust Thou Art

ASH WEDNESDAY is the occasion of a ceremony which enjoys a curious popularity among Catholics. Having ashes smeared on your forehead is not meant to be a particularly enjoyable thing; rather the contrary; it is the outward symbol of penance, which was probably used in the reconciling of notorious sinners before it ever came to be applied, on this one day, to the faithful at large. We humiliate ourselves, disfigure ourselves—just what, in the ordinary way, we least like doing. And yet, as I say, I think there is something curiously attractive to most Catholics about this ceremony. Perhaps it takes us back to our childish days when we liked getting dirty for its own sake, and Ash Wednesday was the one day in the year on which we were allowed to get dirty without being sent upstairs to wash. Dust and ashes; let us give them a few minutes' consideration. Of course it sounds rather too obvious a thing to deserve much attention; but really we are getting into such a complicated frame of mind nowadays that the obvious things are coming into their own again. You open your newspaper and find an advertisement which suggests that you should eat bread; or another which asks you whether you have ever tried burning coal on your fire. There really is a certain romantic appeal about familiar words like bread and coal, as you sit huddled over your anthracite stove eating cardboard for breakfast. And in an age like ours, which knows all there is to be known about electrons and protons and things like that, it is a relief, for once in a way, to devote your considerations to a perfectly familiar thing like dust.

The priest says, as he puts the ashes on your forehead, *Memento homo quia pulvis es et in pulverem reverteris,* "Remember, O man, that thou art dust, and unto dust shalt thou return." First let's notice what an admirably short sentiment that is, only nine words in the Latin; we are asked to remember something, but it ought not to be any great feat of memory even for the most sieve-headed of us. *Pulvis sum et in pulverem revertar*—"I am dust, and unto dust I shall return"—the sort of thing you could write on your shirt-cuff before going in for an examination; and yet it contains, in a sense, the whole of philosophy, and what's more it contains, in a sense, the whole of Christian perfection. Several of the saints dated their conversion from the moment when it suddenly occurred to them, "I say, I'm made of dust."

And let's notice one other point, that this statement which the priest makes on Ash Wednesday is a singularly uncontroversial one. It is not particularly Christian, this sentiment, it is not even particularly religious. The heathen poets rub it in, most of them, till we are tired of it; and the people who write angry books against religion are always repeating it to us savagely as if it were a point that has never occurred to us. Whereas if they had read the book of Genesis they would have found it there in front of their noses; dust thou art, and unto dust shalt thou return.

After all, what a lot of dust was raised last century over the evolution business! People went about with long faces cursing Darwin and the other people for tracing man's ancestry, with a certain amount of genealogical license, from some monkey or monkeys unknown. They minded that terribly; not so much, I think, because they were Christians as because in their heart of hearts they were good old solid Victorians, who thought that the human species, as represented by Lord Macaulay, was the highest kind of existence that could possibly be conceived; it was a sort of blasphemy to connect it in any way with the zoo. But if they'd looked in the Bible, instead of being so anxious to defend the accuracy of the Bible, they'd have found something much worse than that. The Bible says the Lord God formed man out of the slime of the earth. That's what we are, Lord Macaulay and all the rest of us, slime. We belong, on the bodily side of us, to the world of matter; are taken out of that common stock-pot from which all the rest of the visible creation comes. We are animals, we are organisms, we are matter—slime of the earth.

True, that is not the whole account of us, although that is where the pagan and the materialist stop. The materialist position is best expressed, as usual, by the old Greeks— "everything is mockery and everything is dust and everything is nothing, for all that is found in existence is made up out of unreasoning things." The fallacy lies in the ambiguous use of the preposition "out of"; because all that we meet with in our experience is *made up out of* irrational material, it is wrongly inferred that all creation *consists of* nothing else. Whereas the sacred author, having pointed out that we are made of dust, proceeds to supplement the impression he has given; God, he says, breathed into man's nostrils the breath of life, and man became a living soul.

I don't think it's necessary to suppose that we are being informed of anything we couldn't have found out for ourselves. The fact is that this universe which is made up of irrational dust bears, nevertheless, the stamp of reason marked upon it; and that man, unique among the creatures, has a reasoning faculty which is akin, evidently, to that higher and immaterial order. Alone among the creatures, man can look back upon himself and become the object of his own thought; can distinguish the world he knows from himself as knowing it. And in the exercise of that faculty, at however low a level, he transcends the limits of mere matter and makes himself one with that higher order of which matter is only the inadequate expression.

Nevertheless, he is dust. This body of yours *is you.* No good to talk, Eastern-fashion, as if the body were a cage in which your soul is imprisoned, or a garment which your soul wears and can slip off at any time. It is all very well as a matter of rhetoric to talk about your body as a garment of dust. But if somebody jabs a pin into you, it is no use telling yourself that it is going into your garment of dust; it goes into you. The liaison, whatever it be, between your body and your soul is something quite unique; we have no comparison, in the whole of our experience, which would begin to make it clearer to us. We are, as a matter of fact, intellectual souls; and those souls, our religion assures us, are immortal. But once we begin to think about ourselves as immortal souls, we are inclined to grow self-important and put on airs about it. So the first way in which we are encouraged to humiliate ourselves, at the very threshold of this penitential season of Lent, is to remember (what is quite equally true) that we are dust—lumps of matter lying about for no very obvious reason in a world which is as material as ourselves.

And there's a further point which the use of that word "dust" seems to me to bring out, though possibly you will regard me as rather fanciful, rather stretching a point, when I allude to it. Sitting here and thinking of you as a set of dust-heaps, the question naturally presents itself, Why don't you blow away? King David says of the wicked, "Let them be as the dust before the face of the wind"; and we are all fairly wicked, yet we don't blow away, why is that? The point is, of course, that we owe to God not only our creation in the first instance but our conservation, as it is called —we are held in being only by a continuous exercise of his will. So if you will remember that you are dust you will not only be humiliated by the thought of your origin, the base clay from which you sprang; you will also gain the sense of dependence upon God; you will be sobered and chastened by the thought that every single action of your life—even the sinful actions of your life—could not happen without the concurrence of his will. All this that I've been saying refers, of course, to your soul quite as much as to your body; but, as I say, it's easier to remember the insufficiency of your body, this absurd thing which can become a nuisance to you whenever it has a slight toothache or an attack of indigestion.

Well, after that we begin to need a little comfort. For

the sake of comfort, let us turn to a passage in the Psalms which is, perhaps, the most comforting text in the whole of the Bible. The 102nd Psalm tells us that "as a father hath compassion on his children, so hath the Lord compassion on them that fear him; for he knoweth our fashioning, he remembereth that we are dust." He remembers it; he doesn't have to be reminded of it once a year on Ash Wednesday, he remembers it all the time.

Oh, I suppose it's obvious enough, because after all he knows everything. But, put like that, it always seems to me like a glimpse into the Mind of God. Every time the door of the confessional opens, a cloud of dust blows in—that's how God sees it. He knows our fashioning, all the odd little kinks and flaws in our make-up that make us easier victims for this or that bad habit; all the circumstances of every action of ours, the exact provocation we had, the exact strength of the temptation that assailed us. We often try to explain matters to him in the confessional; point out that we were taken off our guard, didn't really think what we were doing—he doesn't need to be told, he knows all that.

Some of us, no doubt, are inclined to take our sins too much for granted, especially when we often fall into the same sins. But there are others who tend to lose heart when they find themselves falling so often; worse still, lose their temper and get angry with themselves, the worst possible disposition in which you can go to confession. Those people ought to remember, as God remembers, that they are made of dust; there is nothing really surprising about it if we, whose fallen nature is what it is, have to confess frequently that we have come short of God's grace. And all of us ought to remember our dustiness more than we do; it's because we forget it that we become neglectful of our prayers, careless about living, as we ought to live, in God's presence. Our nature is so fickle that it no more tends to stay put than dust in a strong draught. It's all wrong, it must be all wrong, to take to your knees every now and then, and say a whole string of Hail Mary's, when somebody's ill at home or when there's an examination coming off, and imagine that you can work on your own steam all the rest of the time. We are wanting God's grace at every turn; if he is to make anything of us, we have got to learn to live in his presence.

And to help us to do that, the Church gives us one more consideration to turn over in our minds on Ash Wednesday. "Dust thou art, and unto dust shalt thou return." It's not plain dust that is put on our foreheads, but ashes; the ashes of the palms we carried on Palm Sunday the year before; the dead remains, therefore, of something we can remember living and growing and flourishing not so very long ago; the embers of glory. The symbolism of that is plain enough, and, if you will, hackneyed enough. It's all over the heathen poets. Once more, the materialist comes up to us bursting with an argument which he thinks we shall find desperately embarrassing, and discovers that we are using it already. He bids us reflect how short life is, as evidence for the view that nothing really matters. He finds us already insisting on the shortness of life, as evidence that each single moment of it matters enormously.

We are dust, and dust we shall be. The ashes which are smeared over your forehead on Ash Wednesday are a fore-taste, as it were, of the dust that will rattle one day on your coffin. And the Church, with a kind of grim irony, selects spring of all seasons in the year to bring this reminder home to us. Just when garden and hedgerow are beginning to put out the first shy promise of green, when the birds are thinking about building their nests, and the mornings grow lighter, and the sun lingers before setting, and there are signs of a fresh vigour in the blood, and we seem to have got rid of the last of our winter colds, and altogether we begin to think things are not so dusty after all, the Church suddenly plucks us by the sleeve and says, "Remember, you are dust." This body of yours, with whatever graces endow it, with all that it has attracted to itself of earth, is destined at last for the charnel-house. All of you that belongs to the body, skill of hand or quickness of eye or strength of muscle, all that of your intellectual faculties, even, which busies itself and is content to busy itself with the things of earth, all the charm you have for others, and the warm memories you have carried away of good days past—all *that* comes from dust and belongs to dust, and you must make your last journey without it. From dust we came, to dust we go; dust we are, unstable and worthless; let us get that into our heads, and we shall begin our retreat in a proper frame of mind.

3 Spring Cleaning

OUR LORD, you will remember, made a sort of spring cleaning of the temple at Jerusalem, when he drove out the traders and the money-changers who were carrying on business there. A retreat should mean that you are having a spring cleaning of your soul, which is meant to be the temple of the Holy Spirit. St. John describes the cleansing in Jerusalem as if it had happened at the very beginning of our Lord's ministry, whereas the other Evangelists describe it as if it had happened just before the Passion. Learned people are apt to talk as if the gospels must have been rather inexact about their dating here; of course, the thing can't have happened twice. I'm not so sure; it seems to me one only needs a very elementary knowledge of human nature to realize that it *may* have happened twice; that two years would be plenty of time for the same old abuses to have crept in again, and have to be dealt with a second time in the same way. That, at least, is what is always happening in these temples of ours, our immortal souls. We go into retreat, and make a really good retreat, and for a time it does really look as if we had had a good clean-up, once for all; the worldliness and self-seeking and the defilement gone, once for all. But it doesn't last long, does it? In two years' time, more likely in one year's time, the same old bad habits have crept back again, and we have to come to our Lord once more to scourge them out of us with the merciful whip of penance. Yes, the temple needed cleansing once in two years; and our souls will need cleaning once in two years at least.

So I want you to look upon this retreat as a kind of spring cleaning; not that in the nature of the case it can be a very thorough spring cleaning, but still, it's a sort of flick round with the duster, and that's better than nothing. We will remember not only the sins that have silted up in our consciences during the last two years; we will go back beyond that and take a look at the weeds which have overgrown our lives from the very start of them, from the first moment when we began to enjoy the use of reason, and see whether we can't catch this year of grace by the skirts as it flies away from us, to make our whole lives, here and now, fit for heaven. That is an ambitious programme; we had better get down to it at once.

First, just let your mind run back over the days or weeks that have passed since your last confession. Is there, perhaps, some mortal sin standing in *that* record, in the live register of your conscience? If so, of course, that's got to be got rid of by confession as soon as possible. Let's just look at that sin for a moment, if it is there. It isn't really part of you. You willed it, to be sure, fully, deliberately; otherwise it wouldn't be a mortal sin. But it doesn't really belong to your nature; it's an excrescence, an adhesion. It has its history in the past; we shall be looking into that in a moment. But you are not to think of it as a matter of course, however much it may have become a matter of habit with you. You forget an engagement, yes, because you are constitutionally forgetful; you overturn a table and break the best tea-things because you are naturally clumsy. But you are not naturally, you are not constitutionally sinful. Naturally, constitutionally, your passions obey your reason, and you do the right thing. True, the equilibrium of the machine, so to put it, is endangered by the results of the Fall. But grace is there, to redress the balance of the machine. The nature that sinned was not your own true nature, but your nature warped, side-tracked, pushed out of shape for the moment. Picture yourself assailed once again by that temptation, and saying No. That is a true picture, true to life; please God it will be true in actual life; why not? Now, let's push that ugly thing away, and start tidying.

You will want to go back over the year or the two years or whatever it was since you made your last retreat. Almost certainly, you will find that retrospect rather discouraging. Rooms that aren't swept get more dusty, not less; shelves that aren't tidied get more cluttered up with things, not less; and the general tendency of your soul or mine is to sink more and more easily into sinful habits, or *rather* sinful habits, from one retreat to the next; it would be vanity if we expected things to be otherwise. If you could draw a graph of a man's spiritual life, I daresay the life of a saint would be a continual, though doubtless not a uniform, curve; yours and mine would be as full of ups and downs as the edge of a saw; there's nothing to be surprised at in that.

Well, I am not suggesting that you should make that

examination here and now. Let this be the recurring burden
of your thoughts, the reflection that offers itself to your
mind when you find yourself, now and again, thrown back
on your own company—What has been my soul's history
since the last opportunity God gave me of coming away and
recollecting myself like this? And in doing that, don't concentrate too much attention upon actual grave sins that
stand out like landmarks—lonely ones, please God—in your
remembrance; try to go deeper than that, and see what has
really been happening to you; how your character has really
been developing, what habits of mind have grown in upon
you, during this last lap of your earthly race.

And the way I am suggesting you should do that—there
is no earthly reason why you should follow out the plan if
it doesn't appeal to you—is to set before you the picture of
our Lord scourging the traders out of the temple, making a
clean sweep of all the things that didn't belong there, in
preparation for that great Sacrifice which was about to be
performed, the one Sacrifice to which all the temple sacrifices looked forward.

Let us just remind ourselves that what these traders were
doing wasn't anything in itself wrong, though no doubt
some of them were unscrupulous about their way of doing
it. Pilgrims were coming to the temple from all over the
world, and you couldn't expect them to come driving their
own sheep with them, or trailing a couple of turtle-doves
on a string; they had got to buy what they needed for the
sacrifice. And the money in which the temple contributions
were made was Jewish money, whereas they came from
parts of the world which used different currencies, so it was

quite necessary to have *bureaux de change* somewhere on the spot. *Somewhere* on the spot, yes, but not just there, not right inside the courts of the temple itself. And I suppose they knew that, or they wouldn't have submitted so tamely to being expelled. What had happened was that, since the last time they were expelled from these courts, they had been creeping in, closer, closer, each one anxious to set up his booth where it would save the customer most trouble. And in that competitive process, first one and then another would cross the sacred threshold, the line beyond which, in reality, he had no right to go. They weren't doing something in itself wrong; they were doing something in itself right and necessary, but without regard to the due limits which ought to have circumscribed the doing of it.

Well, it's not difficult to see how the same consideration applies to our own souls, God's temples, and to that spring cleaning of them which we are trying to undertake. All God's creatures are good in themselves, and sin only lies in the way in which we make use of them, the want of measure and proportion of which we are guilty in our enjoyment of them. Our affections for other people are good and noble in themselves, as long as we have regard to our own state of life and that of the other people concerned. To make money, to make our own living, is a good thing in itself; to enjoy ourselves, to relax after the strain of work or anxiety, is a good thing in itself; to keep up our strength with food and drink is a good thing in itself; to educate our minds, to love beauty and to take an interest in the thoughts which other minds are expressing, in art, in literature, on the stage, and so on, is a good thing in itself. The secret of living according to God's will for us lies precisely in discovering the measure, the proportion, in which he wants you or me to enjoy all these good things, suitably to our state of life and our special needs. How are we going to find a canon, a rule of thumb, by which to test the use we are making of them?

The test which I suggest your applying is that of your prayers. When you are feverish, there are all sorts of effects which that state of health produces, but the simplest test and the most unfailing is that of the thermometer. So, if you begin to suspect, as most of us I am afraid have good reason to suspect, that you are giving yourself up to a feverish enjoyment of God's creatures, the simplest and the most unfailing test is that of your prayers. You *mean* to go to Mass so often, to Communion so often; *do* you? You mean to say your prayers night and morning, to make a daily examination of conscience; do you? If not, what is crowding it out? Late hours, irregular habits, idleness, forgetfulness, moodiness, human respect, want of faith, or what? Again, what happens in your times of prayer? You are distracted; of course you are; everybody is. But what kind of distractions are they which mostly turn your mind away from God? What light do they throw on the things which are meaning, perhaps, too much in your life? You get discouraged; we all do at times. But that discouragement, does the root of it perhaps lie in you; your pride, your selfishness, your vanity? You find prayer distasteful; does that perhaps mean want of generosity on your part; that you are refusing to mould your life on God's pattern, forcing it out of shape by insisting on having it your own way? Somehow or another, the clamour of the world has broken in on that secret enclave of prayer, which is meant to shut you in with God. You need that scourge of small cords that our Lord used to cleanse the temple with; little resolutions, each one of them not costing you much, whose united force will keep the world's traffic at bay.

Positive resolutions, rather than negative ones; resolve, not to see less of this or that person whose society is disedifying to you, but to see more of other friends, whose more salutary influence you have neglected; resolve, not to discontinue this or that dangerous habit, but to find some more useful, some more innocent employment for your time; resolve, not to switch off your interest from some dangerous subject, but to make your interests wider, more representative, more serious than before.

I've still got this spring-cleaning idea running in my head; how are we to represent to ourselves, in those terms, the influence of our old sins; I mean sins which have been forgiven long ago in the confessional, and lie so far in the past that they have ceased to affect our present outlook at all? Let's think of them as those damp patches which you sometimes get on a wall or a ceiling, not doing any harm exactly but just disfiguring it. The roof has been mended where the damp used to come in, so that they are not the signs of any existing unhealthy condition; the whitewash has been put over them again and again, but always mysteriously they reappear. So with those old sins; they have ceased to have any influence on our lives, passed away, perhaps, from memory, but the mark of them is still there, on our record. They have been forgiven in the confessional; but the mark of them is still there, on our record. And those dark shadows on our record will one day be cast onto the screen of eternity; and that will be our Purgatory. They will only be obliterated, in so far as we have atoned for them in this life by offering to God our sufferings and labours here; and some of this satisfaction which we make is stamped with the hall-mark of Holy Church, it takes the form of indulgences. All that we know.

But the Church talks also of plenary indulgences! The whole record wiped out with a single stroke of the pen; is that possible? Some of us can look back on years spent, almost every hour, in committing some offence against God. Is all that to be wiped out? Yes, but if we are to gain the indulgence in full we must not only, as we saw, be in a state of grace, but have an aversion from all our sins, even our venial sins. I wonder how many of us really have that?

And if we haven't got it, how are we going to get it? Well, I am not attempting to lay down the law about what degree of aversion it is that the Church requires of us. But what I am going to suggest is, that in order to feel *sure* we are in the way to gain a plenary indulgence, what we must aim at is nothing less than a complete renunciation of our past life, and of the whole principle on which it has been lived. We have lived, haven't we, selfishly; always, except in a few moments of fervour, or in the case of one or two people we were fond of, putting self first; we have been ungenerous in our dealings with God, doing a little for him grudgingly, and anxiously claiming our reward. All that has eaten into us, lives with us still, that habit of selfishness which has been at the root of our sins and is going to lead us into fresh sins. Can we be *certain* we have the aversion which the Church asks of us, unless we are really turning our backs on that *habit* of selfishness which so obscures our outlook, so distorts our values, makes sinful men of us all the time? And that can be done, how? Only by throwing ourselves absolutely, without reserve, into the arms of God's Providence; willing only henceforth his will for us, not our will; wanting only his glory, not our happiness or peace of mind; annihilating ourselves, and holding ourselves prepared to let God do everything in us, now and always— if we could do that, we could perhaps be *sure* of our plenary indulgence.

4 The Love of God

SHALL WE venture to make a meditation on the love of God? Such a vital subject, for where should we be, if God didn't love us? And what use are we, if we don't love God? And yet a difficult subject, terribly difficult. The love of God, St. John tells us, resides "not in our showing any love for God, but in his showing his love for us first," and again, "Yes, we must love God, he gave us his love first."

It all sounds so simple, but think for a moment what it involves. If God saw you and me, his sinful creatures, eating our hearts out with unrequited affection for him who is so high above us, so remote, so all-sufficient to himself— then we could understand that he might pity us, and pity is a possible foundation of love. We should have no claim upon him, but we could understand it if goodness like his should condescend to weakness like ours. But it's not like that, you see, it's the other way round. It's God who sets the whole thing in motion, by loving us and asking for our love in return.

Difficult to understand, and not simply because we are sinners. That is a point St. Paul calls attention to, but it is a different point; "as if God meant to prove how well he loves us, it was while we were still sinners that Christ died for us." True enough, but then, God is not limited by time; his regard does not have to travel forwards and backwards, like ours. He can see the saint in the sinner; St. Mary Magdalen, St. Paul, St. Augustine—what he loved in them was not, surely, what they were, but what they were going to be; not what they had made of themselves, but what he was going to make of them. The sinfulness of our nature does not make it unrecognizable; it is still what it was when God made it and saw that it was good. He can still recognize it and love it under all the defilement it has incurred, as surely as the father in our Lord's parable could recognize and love the prodigal son, emaciated and in rags. No, the difficulty is not that God should love us although we are sinners. The difficulty is to see how the phrase "God loves us" has any meaning at all.

You see, whenever *we* use that word "love" in connexion with our ordinary human experience, we mean by it an affection—something which affects us, moves us, takes command of our feelings even when we try to resist its influence. The simplest way to assure yourself of that is to reflect that when we are fond of somebody we are apt to say, "I have a weakness for So-and-so"—a weakness, you can't help yourself; perhaps you imply that So-and-so is not everybody's money, that there are faults which might be found in So-and-so, but you have a weakness for him in spite of it. And when this weakness becomes strong in us, then we are weaker than ever. The love of a man and a woman for one another, the love of a mother for her child, how such a love as that can carry us up to the heights, drag us down to the depths, and we seem powerless to prevent it!

Love isn't something we do, it is something which happens to us; something which gets us down, alters us.

Now, if that is, in our experience, the nature of love, what is the use of saying that God loves us, or loves anything? *He* cannot be affected, he cannot be altered, by anything outside himself; he is all act, all will; must it not be absurd to mention his attitude towards us in the same breath with this human quality which we call love? One is very conscious, I think, of that difficulty, in reading the Old Testament prophets. In trying to do justice to God's changeless fidelity, they are for ever comparing his love for Israel with the love of a man for the bride of his youth.

"What is the law of common life?" says Jeremias. "Let wife that has been put away by her first husband marry a second, can she afterwards return to the first? That were shame and defilement. And thou with many lovers hast played the wanton; yet come back to me, the Lord says, and thou shalt find welcome." When they use the language of human love like that, the prophets are using a metaphor; they are comparing Almighty God to a man whose passion is too strong for him, and we see at once that if you tried to press the comparison literally, it would be a contradiction in terms. It is a metaphor, as we all know, when they talk about Almighty God as being angry; it is equally a metaphor when they talk of him as if he were overmastered by the strength of his own love.

And yet, God loves us; that is not a metaphor. Or do we simply mean that he behaves as if he loved us, sometimes, when he pardons our sins or aids us in our difficulties; just as he behaves as if he were angry with us sometimes, when he visits us with punishment? I suppose if God had left us to get on as best we could by the light of our human reason, with no more knowledge of his nature than what philosophy could give us, we might have to say that. But he has revealed himself, and as part of his revelation he has told us that he loves us—*told* us that he loves us? Rather, the whole of his revelation is, first and foremost, a revelation of himself as a loving God. That love, humanly expressed, which shines forth in the human character of Jesus Christ, is only the translation for us in human terms of what God is really like.

If we doubt that, St. John has got it wrong, and St. Paul has got it wrong, and the whole of the New Testament will have to be rewritten. No, we are sorry not to be able to satisfy the philosophers, who ask us what is the sense of saying that God loves when we admit that his love isn't like human love, and human love is the only love we know. All we can say is that human love, love as we know it, must be only an imperfect expression of the real truth which lies beyond our ken, which does not enter into our imagination at all. We know that there must be a divine love which is unlike our human love as the sun is unlike the paltry lights of earth, and yet is at once the continuation and the source and the explanation of it. We dare not deny the truth because the mirror of it in our own minds is imperfect.

God loves us, and asks that we should love him in return. That seems natural, doesn't it, to you and me; we are accustomed to the language, and the logic can take care of itself. But I think it is good for us sometimes to pause in our tracks, and re-examine these over-familiar phrases. Some

time ago, I had a letter from a very intelligent man, not a
professing Christian, but of the kind that is perpetually
bothering about religion, and perhaps beginning to see the
way a bit clearer as time goes on. One thing (he said) I've
never quite been able to understand—the idea of "loving"
God; it seems such an inappropriate word in the circumstances. When I sat down to answer that letter, I confess
that the objection no longer seemed to me quite so odd as
it had at first sight.

After all, the idea of loving God is almost exclusively a
Christian idea. It wasn't language that came natural to the
heathen; in fact, Aristotle says, "We should hardly expect
to hear of anybody loving Zeus," as if he expected to get
a good laugh from the reader. It's true, we are accustomed
to the sound of that sentence in Deuteronomy, "Thou shalt
love the Lord thy God with all thy heart," but if we regard
such a phrase as characteristic of the Old Testament, we
shall be gravely in error. Loving God is only mentioned
about thirty times in the whole of the Old Testament. We
are often adjured to fear God; that is natural enough, considering what God is and what we are. We are often
adjured to seek God; that is natural enough, considering
how hard it is to find out anything about him. But for the
most part, loving God is New Testament language.

Think once again of love as we know it, love as it is
expressed in common human terms. Isn't it true that love
ordinarily implies a certain kind of equality between the
two people who exchange it; each stands equally in need
of the other; anyhow, each likes to think so? Again, we
do not ordinarily fear and love the same person. Sons love

their fathers, but do they fear them? Not much, since
fathers took to playing bears with them on the nursery
floor. Sons used to fear their fathers, but did they love
them much? It is not so long since they used to call them
"Sir." And I suppose it would create rather a sensation in
the regiment if a subaltern were to address the command-
ing officer in the words, "Sir, I love you." The subaltern's
instinctive reactions, you feel, would be otherwise described. And I can understand, can't you, what was in my
correspondent's mind when he said that "love" seemed an
inappropriate way of describing man's attitude towards his
God. The fact is, you see, that we Christians are the spoilt
children of revelation, and we take it as the most natural
thing in the world that God should want us to love him,
instead of reminding ourselves that it is the most amazing
act of condescension on his part. You will remember Hux-
ley's indignant comment on our Christian habits of devotion, "The power that made the stars and the tiger, to be
called by a pet name!" That God allows us to love him—
even that is a privilege.

But there is worse than that; he doesn't simply allow us
to love him, he asks us to love him. And the ground on
which he puts it is that he loves us. Turn that sentiment
into the currency of ordinary human love, and see how
low the divine condescension has stooped to reach us! You
must love me, because I love you—is there any position
more undignified in common human life than that of the
rejected lover, who still hopes to melt the hard heart of
his mistress by asking her to take pity on him, and return
love for love? Is there anything more embarrassing, more

provocative of contempt, than the sight of such a lover when he goes about exposing his wounded heart for all the world to see, inviting our sympathy because he is unloved? Yet that is the figure under which the divine love expresses itself in the devotion of the Sacred Heart; "the Heart that loves so much, and is loved so little in return."

True, it is a human heart that issues the invitation; but it is a Divine Person who speaks, and it is the Divine Love that he offers us. Make no mistake about it, the unsympathetic visitor to our churches is almost always put off by the Sacred Heart devotion. And it isn't just the rather crude form of art that he dislikes, or the rather rhetorical prayers that we say in that connexion; it's the whole idea that repels him; it seems to him just namby-pamby sentimentalism, the framework of a false theological emphasis. We are making God too human, bringing him too much down to our own level; we are representing him as fondly enamoured of us, hiding away his majesty and his terrors. God asks for our love; he does not supplicate for our pity.

What answer do we make to that? Why, that the image of the Sacred Heart does not represent God as he is in his own nature; it represents God incarnate, the human Christ who laboured and loved and wept. "Jerusalem, Jerusalem, still murdering the prophets, and stoning the messengers that are sent to thee, how often have I been ready to gather thy children together, as a hen gathers her brood under her wings, and thou didst refuse it!" It is God that speaks so, but he speaks as Man; it is his human affections that are engaged, when he weeps over the hard hearts of his fellow-countrymen. If you tell him that it is undignified to go on offering his love where it is not wanted, you will not move him; God did not come to earth to be dignified. But that Divine Love which gives itself to us, and asks for our love in return—you have not fathomed the nature of that, you have seen our Lord weeping over Jerusalem; you have only caught the human overtones of it.

No, that Divine Love which chose us out before the world began, which did not create us and then love us, but loved us first and then created us, claims our love by some higher title than that of mere pity, of mere reciprocity. It draws us, like a magnet, of its own force; our hearts turn to it as the flowers turn towards the sun, not persuaded by reasons, but driven upwards by a native impulse. They were made for God; if we will let him have his way with them, the current of love will flow between us, this way and that, until there is no saying which love it is that attracts the other; we can only compare it to the love of man and woman when two hearts beat as one. We did wrong, perhaps, to say that God asks for our love; he does more, he commands it; "Thou shalt love the Lord thy God with all thy heart." It is the law of our being, it is necessary to the fulfilment of our nature. He loved us first; that is not proposed to us as a motive for loving him; it is offered to us as an explanation of why it is that we are able to love him; why it is that we dare to love him; why it is that (unless some fault of ours comes between) we do love him.

God inspires, authorizes, demands our love; love of what sort?

Not one that has its seat in the feelings, or even that has

any repercussion in the feelings; we shall never begin to understand the love of God until we realize that.

It's quite true, as we were saying just now, that what we ordinarily call love between two human beings is a matter of affection; it is accompanied by an immediate emotional response. A lover walks on air; the room lights up for him when the woman he loves enters it; how long the days seem when, for a while, they are separated! Now, our love of God can be, is sometimes, a felt love. Some of us have experienced before now this overflow of the divine love into our feelings; for a few weeks, for a few months, perhaps, prayer came strangely easy to us; we were almost impatient, sometimes, to be alone with God; we found ourselves eager to do him service by some little sacrifice of time or convenience; the thought of him recurred to our minds, with a strange sense of sweetness, at intervals during the day. For a few weeks, for a few months perhaps; but now, all that seems to have disappeared. We go on saying our prayers, and nothing happens; we get nothing out of them except what we put into them; and that isn't much. We fidget in church, as if we were impatient for Mass to be over; even the most elementary sacrifice we make for him, even going without meat on Fridays, seems like a drudgery. And we say to ourselves, "Yes, I used to love God, but somehow I seem to have stopped."

Watch that tendency; it comes straight from the devil. The tendency, I mean, to talk as if we could measure the intensity of our love for God by the intensity of our feelings about it. I spoke just now of an overflow into our feelings, and I used the word advisedly. It is an overflow,

nothing more; our love of God is something in the supernatural order, and it consists of nothing more or less than
the adherence of our wills to him. If, by consenting to
sinful habits, or by encouraging the occasions of sin, you
are setting up your will against his, then that is different;
then you *are* making a fault in love. But if you are trying
to serve him, even though it is not always a great success;
if you are aspiring towards him, keeping your head up-
stream and taking the strain of being a Christian, then you
are loving God, and every whisper of doubt that you feel
about it comes straight from the devil. If the devil can
make you think that you aren't loving God, it's his best
hope of persuading you to stop loving God; he has no
weapon like despair. It doesn't matter how little enjoyment
you get out of your religion, it doesn't matter how little
progress you seem to be making in the affairs of your soul;
it may all be like dragging a log uphill, every Hail Mary
wrenched from you with an effort, but you *are* loving
God.

I don't say it oughtn't to humiliate us. It *is* humiliating,
that God should have created us, filled the world with
beauty for us, and given us such contentment in his creatures; that God should have redeemed us, opening up to
us a new world of grace with its supernatural and eternal
opportunities, and that we should take it so calmly; that
all the evidences of his love should have been staled for us
by familiarity. After all, even the saints have felt that. St.
Philip Neri, the man of all those ecstasies, all those tears,
yet made it his favourite prayer, "My God, I don't love
you one bit." Let us humble ourselves, by all means, for

being the insensitive creatures we are; let us thank God for
all the lives in which his love makes a more sensible repercussion than it does in ours. But never let us doubt that
somewhere in our natures, too deep to wake any external
echoes, the steady, purposeful flow of his love is finding a
response.

Above all, let us beware of trying to test the value of
our love for God by comparing it with the love of some
human creature who is dear to us. There is a scruple which
tempts us to ask, "When I tell God that I love him above
all things, do I really mean that I love him more than So-
and-so?" The question is a foolish one, because you are
confounding two different kinds of love. Your love for So-
and-so is a thing of the affections; you are attracted, by
beauty, by charm, by common loyalties, by common
memories; it is a sentiment you cannot help, a weakness if
you like to call it so. Your love of God is a blind stirring
at the roots of the soul; there is no comparison. Well (you
say), what if the two loves should conflict; what would
happen? Do not ask what would happen—we are poor
creatures. Ask what you would *wish* to happen; if your
will is to love God above all things, you do love him above
all things; you are still responding, however unfeelingly,
to the unfelt influence of his love.

5 The Presence of God

SOMETIMES, if you look in one of those pious manuals, even if it's meant for children, perhaps telling children how to prepare themselves for confession, you will find the curious direction, "Put yourself in the presence of God." Just like that—what do they expect of us? We *are* in the presence of God the whole time. Perhaps the book only means that the child, at this solemn moment, ought to *remember* that it's in the presence of God, and that is sound enough. Children aren't always little angels in church; and it's quite possible that the child addressed is reading a comic under cover of the pew, where the nun can't see it; or is whispering to the child next door, or making faces across the aisle; by all means remind it that such behaviour is out of place in the presence of God.

But we grown-up people, what do *we* do when we are told to put ourselves in the presence of God? We alter the position of the cushion in front of us, and lay down our spectacles on the book-rest, and tidy our hair and take a look at our watches, and—what then? We haven't forgotten that we were in the presence of God; we always knew we always were. What is the exact force of the direction? What is the next mysterious step which "puts us" in the presence of God?

What I think the book means is not that we are to remember, as a fact, the fact that we are in the presence of God, which is quite an easy thing to do; I think it means that we are to *feel* as if we were in the presence of God, and that is an extremely difficult thing to do.

If I were to say to you, for some rhetorical purpose of my own, "Imagine that we're all on a desert island," you'd be able to do something about it. You've read *Robinson Crusoe* when you were small; you've seen desert islands at the pictures. Some of you, those who have strong visual imaginations, would be able to shut your eyes and see, there in front of you, the reef and the palm-trees, hear the lapping of the waves, smell the salt tang of the sea. Others would have to content themselves with *thinking* about a desert island, building up the picture for yourselves, detail by detail, "Yes, I should be walking along the shore looking for crabs, or climbing up some convenient tree to hang my shirt on it and attract the notice of stray battleships"—that kind of thing.

But you would all be able, after a fashion, to do as you were told. It wouldn't be true, but you could imagine it. Whereas, if I said to you, "Imagine the presence of God," it would be true, but you wouldn't be able to imagine it. A presence unconfined by space, not occupying space, making no impression whatever on the senses; a creative presence, which lends to all its surroundings whatever of reality they possess—"No, no," you say, "stop! I can't begin to imagine it, I can't even bear to think of it, it makes my head go round!" Well, what is the good of trying to put ourselves in the presence of God if it makes our heads go round the moment we attempt it?

It looks as if we had got to say that the presence of God was something quite unconnected with our prayer; as if it were just a fact to be docketed when we fall to our knees, and after that a sort of distraction which we had better keep out of our minds. Obviously that isn't true to the instincts of Christian piety; obviously the holy nun who compiled that book of devotions wouldn't have said, "Put yourself in the presence of God," if it were the worst possible thing to do.

Mightn't we suggest this—that although you can't really imagine the presence of God, or even, without blundering into metaphysics, conceive the presence of God, it may be possible to *feel* the presence of God? After all—we have to use imperfect analogies in matters of this sort—isn't there such a thing as *feeling* the near presence of some human person you are fond of, without taxing either the imagination or the intellect in the process? For instance, a mother whose son has just come home after a long absence, and is now asleep in bed—doesn't the house feel different to her because the spare room is no longer unoccupied? She doesn't need to imagine his face lying against the pillow, she doesn't have to reason with herself and propose motives for being happy about it; there is a glow of contentment pervading her which she has no need to analyse or to itemize; every thought which passes through her mind is coloured and lit up by the splendours of this experience. Or even—so much are we at the mercy of our affections—

even a letter from abroad after a long silence, full of unimportant news and conventional expressions of love, will have something of the same effect on a lonely person; she will go about her work with more zest, and the burdens of life will sit more lightly on her, she could hardly tell you why. Even a scrap of paper can produce, between two human beings, the illusion of nearness. And is it possible that the presence of God, which upholds us and inspires us and bathes us in its influence all the time, should never break through this veil of imaginary distance, and become an experience we can feel?

Of course it does. That's obvious in the lives of the saints, and of a great many mystics who have never been canonized as saints. They had the experience; what exactly it was like, they didn't attempt to describe, because like most things that are really worth having it was indescribable. I suppose we should do it least injustice by saying that it must be like the sense of comfort you and I sometimes derive from the presence of a friend, on a long journey for instance, even when we are not talking to our friend or looking that way. But how we come by it—ah, that is a different matter. Perhaps some of you know that little treatise, Brother Lawrence on the Practice of the Presence of God. He seems to have lived for thirty years or more just as conscious of God's presence as I am this moment of yours, or you of mine. But the word "practice" suggests that he is going to tell you how it is done; and the treatise doesn't, somehow, tell you how it is done; with him, it just happened. I suppose many of us have had an experience rather of the same kind, by flashes; lasting for a few moments at a time, and spread out, perhaps, over a series of days or of weeks. It was a grace, nothing perhaps very extraordinary, but it came and went, not at our summons. We could not recapture it by any effort of the will; we could only wait for it to come back again. We still don't know how to *put ourselves* in the presence of God.

If you look up the *Catholic Encyclopaedia*, which is sometimes a good way of resolving your theological doubts, you will be delighted to find that there is a whole article on the subject. And it seems to find the whole thing quite simple, "To put ourselves in the presence of God, or to live in the presence of God, means to become actually conscious of God as present, or at least so to live as though we were thus actually conscious." There seems to be a slight catch about that, doesn't there? Because it talks about being conscious of the presence of God and behaving as if you were conscious of the presence of God as the same thing; but it isn't the same thing. If you are driving a car, it's one thing to be conscious that there is a police car behind you, and quite another to behave as if you thought there was. I'm conscious of breathing; that's to say, I don't attend all the time to the fact that I'm breathing, but I can, so to speak, put myself in the presence of my own breathing, by thinking about it; if I think about it, I feel my chest going up and down. What we want is the power to become conscious of the presence of God by an act of the will, as I can make myself conscious of my own breathing by an act of the will. But all the book gives you is a direction for behaving as if you were conscious of the presence of God, which is quite different. When I refuse to drink water out of the duck-pond, I behave as if I were conscious that it is full of bacteria; but I'm not conscious of anything of the kind, I can't see the bacteria. It's not the same thing.

Of course, what the book was trying to do was to give us a recipe for avoiding sin. But do let's try to get out of the habit of thinking that religion is a dodge for avoiding sin. When you and I talk about the presence of God, we are talking about our prayers. We are wondering whether there isn't some way of making ourselves realize, when we are on our knees, the fact, which we know perfectly well for a fact, namely that God is there. If we could only realize that, we tell ourselves, our prayer would be less disappointing to us, and perhaps to him.

We don't know much about the nature of God, and what we do know is terribly remote, terribly elusive. But still, we do know something, partly from natural philosophy, partly from revelation. Can't we somehow mobilize that knowledge, so that the idea of God, always present, will sink into us? Rather in the same way—I'm afraid I'm giving you a lot of very undignified illustrations, but it can't be helped—rather in the same way as thinking a great deal about illness makes one feel ill. You know how going through a hospital ward, or meeting an old lady who delights in telling you all about her symptoms, leaves you wondering whether you are feeling quite up to the mark yourself; how the very mention of the word "mumps" can make you feel as if you had got a slight swelling on the jaw? All that, you will say, is mere imagination, but in a sense it's more than that; our health, if you come to think of it, *is* precarious, and the very thought of the innumerable ways in which this complicated machinery of ours can go wrong is sufficient to remind us how complicated, and how liable to misfire, that machinery is. Isn't it possible for the mere thought of God to remind us how near we are to God, just as the thought of disease can remind us how near we are to disease?

Well, if I offer some considerations about this, please let it be understood that I'm only putting the case as it seems to me, and with no desire of inflicting my own preferences or habits on you. We are so differently made, aren't we; and even in a simple thing like prayer the differences come out. For instance, tell me this—do you normally pray with your eyes shut, or with your eyes open?

It would make a very interesting subject for those mass-observation people who are always sending out questionnaires to a cross-section of the population. I think it would be found that on the whole Catholics pray with their eyes open, and non-Catholics with their eyes shut; though why this should be so I don't know, because non-Catholics haven't, as a rule, nearly so many ugly things to look at when they keep their eyes open in church. But this difference isn't, I think, a mere difference of tradition, or a mere nervous trick; it is a symbol—you make a gesture when you pray with your eyes open, and you make a gesture when you pray with your eyes shut, and both gestures are perfectly normal and perfectly legitimate.

When you pray with your eyes shut you are, in effect, saying something like this: "My God, I am very grateful to you for all your creatures, but they are a terrible distraction to me. They keep on battering at the gates of sense, and I find myself attending to them instead of attending to you. So I am going to make a gesture by keeping my eyes shut; that gate, at least, shall be barred against distractions; I will try to think only about you."

And if you pray with your eyes open, you are saying something like this: "My God, I know that you have ordained your creatures to lead me to you. I cannot declare that any one of them exists without declaring, in the same breath, that you exist, since they could not exist without you. They are all close round me here, and in every one of them you, by your creating and sustaining activity, are therefore present. Let me read you in them; just as I can look at black ink-marks on a page, and read in them without effort the thoughts of the writer who committed them to paper, so let me look now at my hand here, at the chair it rests on, and read in them your presence."

Those are two quite legitimate attitudes. Don't, please, mistake me; I am only suggesting that they are *symbolized* by keeping one's eyes shut and keeping one's eyes open; I am not suggesting that you, who pray with your eyes shut, are approaching God in this way, or that you, who keep your eyes open, are approaching him in that. But I do think this—that most of us, whatever happens to our eyes, will find it easier to approach God in the second of those two ways; to find him *in* his creatures, rather than to find him by forgetting his creatures. For one thing, they are so difficult to forget; to shut one's eyes is only to conjure up a set of pictures in the imagination not at all less distracting than the pictures we receive through the sense of sight. For another thing, you and I are so curiously made that we can't, if I may use a rather hideous modern expression, face up to the thought of God. We have to think about something else, and look at God, as it were, out of the corner of our eyes. Let me explain.

If you go out into the garden on a bright, sunny day, you don't look up at the sun and exclaim, "How beautiful the sun is!" You look round you at the flowers, at the dew on the grass, at the trees just in bud over there on the hillside, and exclaim, "How beautiful everything looks, in the sun!" That is what I am suggesting about the beginning of our prayer; about that moment at which the books say, "Put yourself in the presence of God." With the utmost deference, I should like to amend that formula, and make it read, "Put yourself in the presence of something else, and find God there."

All I'm saying is that it's not necessary, at such moments, to make a determined act of the will and banish your distractions—even if you know how to do that, which is more than I do. You can look hard at your distractions, and make them melt away into that background, which is God. For instance, your eyes are caught by the flowers on the altar, and you say to yourself, "Good gracious, here am I with only a few minutes to spend in church, and I start thinking about flowers!" No, don't say that; think about the flowers and let them take you to God. That one on the left is drooping rather; they'll all be drooping soon—what a short time flowers last! Flowers? So do we, for that matter; what was it the Greek poet said when he sent a wreath to the girl he was in love with? "Girl and garland, both must bloom and both die." And then your mind travels back to yourself as part of this impermanent world, and then it travels off again outwards, and sees as the background, as the obverse of all this impermanence, that eternal being which is God's. Eternal God, brought near to me in the sight of a flower on the altar—you have not really been wasting your time. Your mind has only been like an aeroplane, taxiing before it can be airborne.

And it is so, of course, not only with those outward things which distract the senses, but with those memories that haunt the mind, and are not to be dispelled by shutting your eyes. You've been criticized by somebody, not with the intent but with the effect of wounding you; it has touched you on the raw; you resent it, and at the same time you aren't quite sure that it wasn't justified. This grievance of yours you must surely expel from the mind, if you are to settle down to prayer. Once more, if you can banish it, do by all means; but it isn't easy. Better, perhaps, to look at the criticism merely *as* a criticism, not going over the ground of your grievance all over again, but just putting it where it belongs, among the criticisms we fallible human beings pass on one another. Even if they're true, we can't be sure they are true; we are so blind, so partial, there is so much that is hidden from us. There are things which will actually never be known; who wrote the Casket Letters, or who was the man in the iron mask; since the truth about such things can never be known, can we really say there *is* a truth about them? Yes, there is a truth about them, because it exists in the Mind of God. And that criticism I was thinking about just now—what was it? I've forgotten—rings true in the mind of God, or rings false. If we were wounded by a chance remark, it was because he wanted it to bring us back, on the rebound, to him.

Don't imagine that I'm suggesting anything easy, anything commonplace. I'm only wondering whether we couldn't, in that sort of way, invite God to us in his presence oftener than we do?

6 The Holy Spirit

IF A MAN should set out to go through the Bible, pausing and making a meditation wherever he found material, his attention would be caught without fail, I think, by the second verse of it. "Earth was still an empty waste, and darkness hung over the deep; but already, over its waters, stirred the breath of God." Creation still in the melting-pot, so that we have nothing for our composition of place except a formless sea of undifferentiated matter; dark, not by some effect of shadow, but with that primal darkness that reigned before light was made. And over this inert mass, like the mist that steals up from a pool at evening, God's breath, his Spirit, was at work. Already it was his plan to educe from this chaos the cosmos he had resolved to make, passing up through its gradual stages till it culminated in the creation of Man.

Deep in your nature and in mine lies just such a chaos of undifferentiated matter, of undeveloped possibilities. Psychology calls it the unconscious. It is a great lumber-room, stocked from our past history. Habits and propensities are there, for good and evil; memories, some easily recaptured, some tucked away in the background; unreasoning fears and antipathies; illogical associations, which link this past experience with that; primitive impulses, which shun the light, and seek to disguise themselves by a smoke-screen of reasoning; inherited aptitudes, sometimes quite unexpected. Out of this welter of conditions and tendencies the life of action is built up, yours and mine. And still, as at the dawn of creation, the Holy Spirit moves over those troubled waters, waiting to educe from them, with the co-operation of our wills, the entire life of the Christian.

The moment you begin to speculate why you started humming such and such a tune at such and such a moment, or why you dreamt last night of a friend, long dead, who in your dream was alive, you catch some glimpse of the vast network of association there must be below the level of consciousness. Have you ever tried to eradicate sorrel from a garden path? Or even thistles? Those long ligaments which connect one patch of weeds with the next make a good image of what mental association must be like, if it could be unearthed to our view. Nowadays, there is so much novel-writing and so much art-criticism which exploits the findings of the psychoanalysts that we are, if it is not too paradoxical to put it in that way, perpetually unconscious-conscious. We are for ever turning in upon ourselves, and scrutinizing the hidden sources of our own conduct.

What I want to suggest, in giving you a meditation about the action of the Holy Spirit on our lives, is that there is a further, rather interesting parallel between the chaos out of which the world was formed and the chaos which underlies consciousness. In the seventeenth and eighteenth centuries, when the discoveries of the scientists, and of Newton in particular, had dominated men's minds with the notion of order and mechanical sequence in the world of nature around us, the thought of the day became infected with a tendency which we remember under the name of Deism. Philosophers who believed, sincerely enough, that the existence of the universe could only be attributed to a creator, restricted his rôle to that of a creator and let it stop there. He had made (these people told us) a piece of mechanism so flawless in its construction that it could roll on its course by means of some self-regulating principle without any further interference. How they managed to remain satisfied with such a naïf doctrine, it is difficult to see. Nobody who contemplates Michael Angelo's picture of the creation of Adam can fail to be impressed by the gesture of the outstretched arm, which seems to suggest that Adam is just letting go; how far, we wonder, and in what sense was it possible to let go? But I am not concerned to discuss the difficulties of the theory; only to point out that there has *been* a theory, held by people who were Christians after a fashion, which left no room for the divine conservation, left no room for miracles or the intrusion of the supernatural; which regarded the whole of creation as a mere *fait accompli*, set in a mould.

And, if you come to think about it, that is exactly the danger which the new psychology has for you and me. It tends to make us think of ourselves as set in a mould, certain to react in this or that fashion to this or that stimulus, because that is the way we are built. Or rather, that is the way we have got warped, by the impressions we get in extreme youth, long before we've attained the use of reason. The first seven years of our lives are like the seven days of creation, the only really formative period; after that, nothing will make any difference—except perhaps going to a psychoanalyst. Oh, we go on fighting against our temptations, but with the feeling that the dice are loaded against us; we are obeying the call of something so deep down in us that we can't get at it—that is the frame of mind we find ourselves in, when we have been coming across this modern talk about psychology.

If you want to get a complete reversal of the eighteenth-century Deist approach, you have to go back to the Middle Ages. How splendidly the medieval people took everything in their stride! To them, the constant stir and motion in the world around them was the work of the Holy Spirit—the rustling, as it were, of his passage; that "the spirit of the Lord fills the whole world" was as clear to them as to the author of the Book of Wisdom. So it was that Adam of St. Victor wrote, in his hymn *Qui procedis ab utroque:*

> "Love, that equally enchainest
> Son and Father, Love that reignest
> Equally, of both the peer,
> All things fillest, all things lovest,
> Planets guidest, heaven movest,
> Yet unmoved dost persevere."

They, no less than the men of the eighteenth century, were impressed by the movements of the celestial bodies, but to them it was something alive, not something mechanical.

Well, I suppose they were naïf about their science, just as the men of a later age were naïf about their philosophy. But I always feel that we have lost something, we modern Catholics; something of that splendid boldness with which the medievals treated all experience as one. We think of the Holy Spirit, don't we, as concerned with us men, as helping us in our decisions, as quickening us with more fervour of devotion; we do not feel the draught of his impetuous movement in the world around us. We are all so scientific.

Well, be that as it may, we have got to believe, on pain of heresy, that the Holy Spirit does interfere, all the time, in your life and mine; that his influence plays over us, like the steady breeze which fills the sails of a boat, or like the sudden gusts which send the autumn leaves spinning in the air. At least, I don't know that that is really a very good comparison. Because the wind catches the surface of things; when it is blustering on the hill-tops you may be sheltered from it in the valley. Whereas it is a plain fact of experience that the operations of the Holy Spirit do not manifest themselves on the surface; they take effect within. They belong to that hidden self of which we have been speaking, the self that lies below the level of consciousness. Below? Perhaps above; but at least beyond the range of our knowing. When you stand in face of some important decision, when (for example) you are electing your state of life, you naturally invoke the aid of the Holy Spirit. But, having done that, you proceed to make up your mind exactly as you would have made it up in any case; by weighing arguments, by taking human advice, and so on. You do not expect a sudden illumination from heaven to break in upon your

calculations. Even on those rare occasions when a salutary
thought strikes you quite out of the blue, with no previous
train of thought to account for it, you say, perhaps, "It was
an inspiration"; but then you reflect, "How can I be certain
of that? How do I know what hidden association of past
memories may have set my brain working in that way? Perhaps it wasn't an inspiration after all." But it *was;* there's
nothing to prevent the Holy Spirit using some association of
past memories in your brain-cells to produce the effect he
wanted. The breath of God stirred over the turbid waters of
your unconscious self, and said, "Let there be light."

What I'm trying to suggest is that most of us have a
rather limited view about the help we expect to receive
from the Holy Spirit. Our devotion to him is real, but it is
something that we keep for special occasions; moments of
vital decision, or acute spiritual crisis. It is so easy to think
of yourself as a boat propelled by machinery, which can
get along all right most of the time by its own power—it's
only when the engine breaks down that you bother to hoist
the sails. When I used to teach at Old Hall you would get
summoned, now and again, to some meeting of professors to
discuss College business; and you put your pipe in your
pocket on the chance; but if the meeting began with *Veni
Creator Spiritus* you knew that you might just as well have
left it behind. I don't want to criticize my old college, but it
did and does seem to me that there's a slight tinge of Jansen-
ism about the idea that if you light a pipe the Holy Spirit
ceases to take any further interest in your deliberations. We
forget, you see, how constant and how intimate is the play
of his influence on our lives. But why should we? We've

lost, no doubt, the medieval trick of tracing it in the movements of the heavens, but surely we ought to trace it in the mysterious movements of our own minds, stirring over that primeval chaos which underlies the cosmos of our daily thoughts?

It isn't true, and of course it can't be true, that only the impressions of early childhood have the power to mould a man's character. On the contrary, we are building it up all the time; from hour to hour the complicated tapestry of our lives is being woven out of fresh material. We are accustomed to remember that, when it is a question of the will making some conscious decision—consenting, for example, to sin. Every sin, the spiritual authors hasten to assure us, diminishes in some tiny degree our capacity to resist the next temptation. But, you see, it isn't only our moral choices or even our conscious thoughts that have this power to affect us; all the time we are taking in something from our surroundings. Just as our bodies are exposed, day by day, to a hundred dangers which we cannot see, so our minds can be influenced by things which don't seem to matter; sights and sounds that were hardly registered, impressions which at the time had no moral significance, no taint of sin and no relish of salvation in them, can leave their mark ever so slightly, and help to make us, for better or worse, the people we are.

I'm not saying this to frighten anybody or make anybody scrupulous; I'm only trying to point out that when you and I invoke the Holy Spirit we are not just inviting him to be there in case of accidents. We are recognizing that there is a whole world of minute mental happenings which, but for his watchful care, may turn to poison for us. We are asking him to guide us, not only in the momentous choices which seem to us important, but in every tiny decision of our wills, because the effects, even of such a decision, may have results beyond our knowing. One has heard of sectaries who would not even cross the street without asking for guidance; we may laugh at their scruples, but we have to admit that they are distortions of a true principle.

Don't let us be content, then, to ask the aid of the Holy Spirit in getting the better of our temptations; let us ask him also to do something about this background of sinfulness from which our temptations arise, this chaos of hidden, conflicting tendencies within us which is, which has become, our nature. There is a work of cleansing and of mending to be done in us at a level which escapes our observation altogether. That haunting list in the fourth verse of *Veni, Sancte Spiritus* is not a list of sins; it is a list, drawn up under various images, of those faults in our nature which are the context of our sinning.

Lava quod est sordidum, wash clean what is sordid. What is filthy, if you will; but in our speech that metaphor has a narrow compass; defilement conjures up in our minds the picture of sensual temptations. It is natural that it should be so; dirt is only displaced matter, and those sins in which sex plays a part are only the abuse of a noble thing in our nature. But in the language of the New Testament the word "defiled" has a more general meaning; when St. James, for example, tells us to cast aside all defilement, and all the ill-will that remains in us, he seems to be thinking of that mean streak in our natures which rejoices in taking unfair advantage of an enemy. What is sordid in us is what we ourselves would be ashamed of if it came to light. When you are moved by jealousy to detract from the praises of some rival, that is sordid. When you grudge somebody the help he might expect of you, just because he is a bore and uncongenial to you, that is sordid. Not only from the rebellion of sensual desires, which makes itself clearly felt, but from the meanness which hides itself away under so many cunning disguises, we ask to be delivered when we pray *Lava quod est sordidum*.

Riga quod est aridum, water the parched soil—when we say *that*, we are not thinking only of disabilities which arise from our own fault. There is, as we all know, a dryness in prayer which belongs to a different category. Commonly—I think you can say, most commonly—it is not the result of sin or a punishment of sin, but a discipline which God sends us by way of testing the quality of our love for him. And if we ask the Holy Spirit to lighten that discipline for us, it is only from a salutary fear that we shall not be able to stand the test. But there *is* a dryness in our human contacts which is a defect in us, and often a defect which grows in us. A kind of selfishness cuts us off from our fellow-men; we can't summon up the effort to make friends of people. From this ingrowing selfishness, our fault only in part, we ask that we may be delivered.

Sana quod est saucium, cure what is wounded in us—there we find ourselves talking the language of psychology. Our traumas; the irrational antipathies, the unaccountable phobias which seem to mark us out from our fellow-men—

they have become part of our nature, and we can do nothing about them. *We* can do nothing about them, and therefore we ask the Holy Spirit to heal us, if he will, of these forgotten wounds which so hamper our activity.

Flecte quod est rigidum, bend what is stiff in us; that difficulty of approach which our neighbours find in us, so largely due to mere shyness, mere awkwardness; that unsympathetic attitude towards the failings which we don't evidently share; that self-withdrawal which isn't quite pride but is next-door neighbour to it—we want to be rid of that too.

Fove quod est frigidum—chafe what is numb. Sometimes a kind of torpor creeps over the mind, like the chill of old age, deadening (or so it seems) the faculties of the spirit; our zeal for souls, our hope of salvation, even faith itself, haven't been lost, but it's as if they had been sealed off, like a finger or a foot rendered insensible by frost. What is the explanation of it, where lies the fault in it, and how grave, we cannot tell; but oh, if it could be chafed back to life!

Rege quod est devium—straighten out what is warped. What a curious thing it is, the cross-grainedness, the contrariness of some people; how a man can so want to be different from his fellows that he differs for the sake of differing; enjoys the martyrdom of intellectual loneliness; delights in shocking the prejudices of his neighbours. Oh, it is harmless enough on a small scale, and often amusing; but it is a dangerous kink, not always far removed from pride. If the Holy Spirit would iron out those exaggerated eccentricities, bring us back again to the true!

"The Spirit," says St. Paul, "comes to the aid of our weakness; when we do not know what prayer to offer, to pray as we ought, the Spirit himself intercedes for us, with groans beyond all utterance." Down in the depths of our fallen nature he is at work, re-interpreting us to ourselves, subtly fashioning us, according the measure of the perfect man in Christ—without our knowledge, but not, perhaps, without our asking for it.

7 Our Victim

IT IS A familiar reflection that our modern civilization, and
the newspapers especially, which are the characteristic
product and expression of our civilization, have produced a
decline in the English language. No symptom of that decline
can more readily be observed, than the weakening of certain words, strong, pregnant words by their origin and
derivation, through constant misuse. We are accustomed to
it in everyday speech; words like awful and frightful and
delicious and splendid—good, strong words with plenty of
feeling and plenty of history behind them—have become
almost meaningless. People tried to be emphatic by using
these words to exaggerate their meaning, and the result is
that the meaning of these words themselves has been ob-
scured or lost. They have become trivial; it is no longer
possible to use them in poetry, for example, or in any serious
connexion. Sometimes we see an old-fashioned church with
the words written up over the door, "How awful is this
place"—and we roar with laughter; but, of course, when
that inscription was put up, the words, taken from the Bible,
were solemn and significant enough.

But, as I say, the newspapers have to bear most of the
blame. They are for ever describing a thing as a tragedy

when it is not really a tragedy, only a rather sordid story of
a man who can't pay his bills suffocating himself with a
gas oven; or you will see a love affair between a titled person
and an actress described as a romance, not because there
was really anything romantic about it, but because it fits into
a certain pigeon-hole in the journalist's mind which is
labelled, for no particular reason, "romance." What a noble
word is the word "ordeal"—the judgement of heaven, men
exposing themselves to great dangers in the confidence that
Providence will protect their innocence! But now, if a lift
sticks on the tube, all the passengers in it are idiotically
described as having undergone an "ordeal" in the papers
next morning. And the headline in the next column is something about a "vigil," which calls up to your mind pictures
of a knight watching over his arms before the altar of a
church, but refers, you find, to a lot of people who got up
at five in the morning to queue up at the box-office of a
new play.

I've been thinking lately, how terribly this process of
depreciation has affected another familiar word, the word
"victim." It is almost as bad as the word "martyr"; but
whereas we are still conscious that the word martyr is being
used in a violently metaphorical sense when somebody is
described as a martyr to kidney trouble, we have got so accustomed to the misuse of the word victim that we have forgotten what its original significance was. When a few
hundred people are driven from their homes by an earthquake, they are described as earthquake victims; when somebody is knocked down with a life-preserver we call him the
victim of a murderous attack. But you can't be the victim

of an earthquake, or of a murderous attack. To be a victim means essentially to suffer punishment in somebody else's stead; to undergo suffering which you haven't deserved in order that somebody else, who has deserved it, may go free. And that is what we mean when we speak of our Lord as a Victim; or describe his Body, present in the Holy Eucharist, as the Host or Hostia. He was not the Victim of crucifixion; he was not the Victim of the Jews. He was *our* Victim; suffered for us in order that our punishment might fall upon him.

So much, even his murderers realized. It is expedient (said Caiphas) that one man should die, and not that the whole people should perish. He did not know that the Holy Spirit was prophesying through his lips; he only meant that the murder of our Lord would save Judaea from the terrible consequences of a popular rising against the Romans. But he did see Jesus of Nazareth, and seeing him, half pitied him, as the victim of his people. Blind master of the law, how was it that the words of the prophet Isaias never came to his memory; "truly he bore our griefs, and himself carried our sorrows . . . he was wounded for our iniquities, ground to pieces by our crimes . . . all of us have wandered away like sheep, each has followed his own path, and the Lord has laid the iniquity of all of us upon him. He was offered up because he himself willed it . . . for the sin of my people I have smitten him"? All that Caiphas forgot; but he knew what a victim was.

He was offered up because he himself willed it; that is the point of Good Friday. He was dumb as a sheep before his shearers; but whereas the sheep is dumb because it is too foolish to see the knife, or too helpless to make any gesture of resistance, our Lord knew all the time what was coming, could at any moment have averted it, and still he was dumb, and still he gave himself to the knife. Let us try to follow the story of our Lord's Passion as if we were reading it for the first time, and didn't know what was going to happen at the end of it. Let us observe how, from the dramatic point of view, the development of the plot is exactly what we should not have expected; tragedy would have demanded that circumstances should be too strong for the hero, and that he should have been swept unwilling to his fate—but our Lord was in full control of all the circumstances all the time. Let us observe how historically there was no reason at all why our Lord should have fallen into the hands of his enemies even if he had only been a man, using common prudence and common weapons of defence. Let us observe how, as God, he could have interfered with the process at any moment, and he never interfered. It was the victim's part that he had chosen.

First of all, he knew exactly what was going to happen. He prophesied three times that he was to be crucified by the Gentiles; and when his favourite apostle was scandalized at the very mention of such an idea, he turned upon him and addressed him as Satan—the only time he ever addressed that word of reproach to a human being. Yet, for a time, it looked as if he was not going to let the malice of his enemies have a chance; when they had determined on his death, he did not stay in Judaea, where he was at their mercy, but withdrew himself beyond Jordan. Then we find him in Galilee, where he was safe among his own people;

and it looks as if he was not going up to Jerusalem for the passover, so conscious is he of danger. Then the message comes that Lazarus is ill in Bethany; and he has to go into Judaea to visit him and to save him. Then, surely, he is running into danger; his apostles realize that well enough; "Let us all go," says St. Thomas, "and die with him"; the pessimist of the party, he has no doubt about the issue.

But it doesn't quite work out like that. Our Lord reaches Bethany unmolested; and when he does go into Jerusalem, it is as the prophet who raised Lazarus from the dead; he is escorted into the city in a triumphal procession. He preaches in the temple, but he does not stay in Jerusalem; night after night he goes back to Bethany, and spends the evening safely with his friends. Then, on the Thursday night, he changes his plans. He will stay the night in Jerusalem, and eat a paschal meal with his disciples. Notice that he is under no obligation to do anything of the kind; the real paschal supper did not take place till the Friday, and if he had eaten the paschal meal on Friday he would have been safe enough; no Jew could lift a hand against him once the feast had begun. But no, of his own accord he will spend Thursday night in Jerusalem; and that is the fatal moment. Is it, perhaps, that he doesn't realize what dangers he runs; doesn't realize that there is treachery within his own camp? On the contrary, he knows that there is treachery, publishes the name of the traitor, and invites him to make haste with his abominable project. Judas leaves the supper-table and now —now, surely, is the chance to escape. Easy to reach Bethany before the temple guard can be summoned to arrest him. Or at least he can remain in hiding; if he will

leave the cenacle, neither Judas nor anybody else will know
where he has gone. He *is* leaving the cenacle; ah! then it
will be all right. But no, he goes out to the precise spot
where Judas will be most likely to look for him, the garden
of Gethsemani. It is as if he had made a special assignation
with the traitor for the very purpose of giving himself up.

Yet he travels with an escort, and two out of that escort
are armed with swords. He comes into the garden, and prays
—prays that the cup of his Passion may be removed from
him. Surely, if ever a prayer was worthily offered, if ever a
prayer deserved to be granted, it was this! And still the
heavens are dumb, and the torches of the high priest's
servants draw nearer through the trees. One blow is struck,
and then the sword must be put back into its sheath again;
after all, there is to be no resistance. And yet, what need for
such resistance by armed force? Have we not seen the
defenceless Prisoner quell his captors with a word, so that
they all went backwards and fell to the ground? Yes, but he
takes no advantage of their panic; waits there patiently, and
gives himself into their hands. He is so confident, it seems,
in the justice of his cause that he is determined to be led off
to trial; will they really be able to condemn him as a male-
factor, when he has given such proof of his peaceable inten-
tions?

The trial begins, and once again it looks as if everything
must be all right. Even such judges as these will hardly be
able to pronounce a conviction when the witnesses for the
prosecution are contradicting one another. . . . The Prisoner
himself remains silent, until the high priest, with a flagrant
disregard of all legal process, challenges him with the very

question that is at issue, Is he the Son of God or not? He has every right to remain silent, but he speaks; and in speaking he ruins his own cause; "I am." But the proceedings have dragged on; it is early morning now, and the chief priests, if they are to succeed at all, must get a conviction by night-fall. At six in the evening, the sabbath begins, and they will not be able to take any further action. How they must have chafed and fumed as the long interrogation went on, before Herod and Pilate, when every minute was precious to them! And indeed, it seems doubtful whether Pilate can be induced to pronounce sentence of death. He finds no cause; his wife intercedes with him to show clemency; why should not the Galilean, rather than Barabbas, be reprieved, this feast-day? Why should not Pilate scourge him and let him go? The Prisoner is silent again, though now what he needs for his defence is speech, not silence; when he speaks, once more it is to make the most damaging admission possible; he claims to be a king! This is he, who again and again put his enemies to shame by his quick answers; and now, on trial for his life, he loses every advantage in turn.

What is the meaning of all that pageant (so it seems) of mismanagement? Simply that he will remind us at every point what his attitude is; the attitude of a willing victim. There are angel legions ready to succour him to the last, but he waves them back. He chooses suffering; when, out of mercy, the soldiers offer him wine mingled with gall, a rude anaesthetic for the pain of crucifixion, he will but taste it in acknowledgment of their charity; he will not drink. And, as if it were not enough that we should have a single example of this victim-attitude of his, he will share it with another. Our Lord, remember, had only just come down from Galilee to help Lazarus; he knew what was going to befall him in Judaea. What would have been easier for him than to leave his Blessed Mother at home, so that she could have been spared all her anguish, heard of the crucifixion and the resurrection from the lips of the same messenger? But no, he will have her with him in Judaea, with him in the cenacle, with him on Calvary. Mankind shall see his victim-attitude reflected, as in a mirror, in her.

In two ways, obviously, that willingness of our Lord to give himself into the hands of his persecutors is concerned with the history of our own lives, as lived in God's sight.

In the first place, our Lord does entrust himself to us, and when we commit sin, we betray, we insult, we defile that divine presence in our souls. There is a sense, indeed, in which every sin of ours is a direct betrayal of God himself. For we sin against him by misuse of his own gifts; and, since no action of ours can take place without the concourse of his will, we are in a sense making him the accomplice of our own misdeeds, as far as it lies in our power to do such a thing, when we act in defiance of his law. We are to think of him, not as a detached Witness of our wrongdoing, but as a Benefactor who is concerned with it; it is as if a rebel should attack his sovereign with the forces which that sovereign has put under his command. But, as we know, the case is worse than that. When we are in a state of grace, our Lord does live in our souls through the power of his Holy Spirit; we betray that condescension of his, we attack that mystical life of his, when we offend against the law of God. Worst of all, because most direct of all, is when his Sacramental Presence is profaned by a sacrilegious Communion, not only our Friend but our Guest betrayed. God puts himself, as it were, at my disposal; Christ gives himself, hands himself over to me; I take my part with Judas, with Caiphas, and with Pilate if I show myself unworthy of his confidence.

That is one application of the Passion to our own lives. The other carries us further still: would our Lord have been at such pains to emphasize his acceptance of the victim-state, if he had not wished to recommend to us, his followers, the same attitude towards suffering? After all, the actual circumstances of the Passion were not the only way in which our Lord's will to die for us could have been accomplished. He could have set the seal of martyrdom on his mission equally well if he had allowed the Jews, when they took up stones to cast at him in the temple, to achieve their design, instead of frustrating it by a miracle. If he had died like St. Stephen, we should still have known that suffering, and the acceptance of suffering, were part of the perfect life as God wishes it to be lived in this imperfect world.

But he would do better than that. Our Lord would show us, in this long drama of our redemption, a divine-human Will confronted at every turn of the road by a choice between suffering and escape, choosing at every turn suffering rather than escape, identifying itself with the Justice that inflicted, though on an innocent Victim, the heavy punishment of our sins. We were to know, not guess merely

but know, that the acceptance of suffering is the key to
this world of mystification in which man lives since he lost
his Paradise. We were to know, not guess merely but know,
that the important question was not, How shall suffering
fall on him who has most deserved it?, but the question,
How shall suffering fall on him who will most accept it?
And, in the light of that knowledge, we were to offer ourselves, each in his own measure, as victims for sin; not each
for his own sins, but each for that common debt of sin
which all of us owe beyond our powers of repayment, fill-
ing up in our bodies that which is lacking of the sufferings
of Christ for his body's sake, which is the Church (Colos-
sians 1:24). Suffering was to mean henceforth not, what
it had always meant hitherto, something negative, sitting
still and waiting for things to happen to you, the opposite
of action, but something positive, the identification in will
of the sinful and sin-laden victim with the Justice of God
manifested in punishment.

Ever since then, at whatever period in history you care
to look, you will find Christian men and women deliberately
inflicting suffering upon themselves, so as to be conformed
to the likeness of Christ; not content merely to shut themselves away from the world and its dangers, not content
merely to live simply and sparingly, so as to avoid the
temptations which luxury brings with it, but actually going
out of their way to hurt themselves; scourging themselves
with the discipline, denying themselves food and sleep,
and so on. Is that, then, the cue for all of us? Ought we all
to choose suffering as our ambition and our career? No,
the mind of the Church is clear on this point, that heroic

mortifications ought only to be undertaken by those comparatively few souls whose special vocation lies that way; and then only in obedience to the control of a director. All the same, I think you can say this—that the life of a Christian who has never denied himself anything for the sake of following our Lord is to that extent an incomplete life, and that such a Christian will be ill trained to bear other sufferings which come to him through no will of his own, as assuredly they will. Would Thomas More have found prison and execution a matter for jesting, if he had not schooled himself by wearing a hair-shirt in the days of his prosperity?

But those sufferings and privations which God sends us, unasked and unsought for—those, if we have studied in the school of the Passion, we shall learn to meet in the attitude of victims. We may remember if we will that there is a debt which still remains to be paid for our own sins, either here or in the next world; and we may content ourselves, if we will, with the grim consolation that what we suffer here will, if we bear it faithfully, cancel some part of the suffering which belongs to us hereafter. But if we have a real aversion from our sins, if we really try to make God, not self, the centre of our world, we shall go, I think, further than that. Hating our sins, we shall hate sin for itself; we shall esteem, therefore, the suffering which is its antidote; having God for the centre of our world, we shall wish away from it all that offends him, welcome, therefore, the suffering which obliterates its consequences.

I am speaking of the will; I don't mean that pain will hurt us or poverty pinch us less than our neighbours. But we shall find it possible to identify our wills with everything that comes to us from God's hands, good or evil; evil rather than good, because it marks us out as his friends. The crucifix will be the clue that disentangles the mysteries of life for us; and in the end, the key that opens the door of death for us. We shall offer ourselves, in life and in death, as our Lady did by the cross, in union with the Sacrifice her Son made; victims with him and through him for the sins of the whole world.

8 The Crucifix

Sᴛ. Jᴏʜɴ tells us that after the raising of Lazarus the chief priests and Pharisees called a council in alarm; if they left our Lord to his own devices (it was pointed out), he would find credit everywhere; "then the Romans will come, and make an end of our city and our race." It was then that Caiphas, the high priest, suggested, "It is best for us if one man is put to death for the sake of the people, to save a whole nation from destruction." All four evangelists report Pilate as asking our Lord, "Art thou the King of the Jews?" but only St. John tells us that there was a time, just after the feeding of the Five Thousand, when there was a popular attempt to make a king of him.

It is easy to see what would have happened if Pilate, if the authorities at Rome, had been faced by a serious attempt to found a new theocratic kingdom in the province of Judaea. The destruction of Jerusalem would have taken place a generation earlier. Caiphas was telling the truth, according to his lights, when he said it was a good thing that one man should die for the sake of the people. The curious thing, as St. John points out, is that he was telling the truth even beyond his lights. He was the high priest, and for a moment the prophetic gift of Aaron flickered in the mind of his unworthy descendant. For the last time, the Urim and Thummim of the old covenant issued a divine decision.

Was ever counsellor so right, and so wrong? Right, assuredly, in seeing that this was no common agitation he was dealing with; that the fire kindled upon earth would spread into a conflagration, if it were not attacked now at its very centre, and extinguished. It is easy to say that persecution always defeats its own ends, and that Caiphas ought to have known it. But does persecution always defeat its own ends? That is, after all, only a pious commonplace invented by the winning side when it looks back on its early days of unpopularity. History is scarred with the record of idealistic movements which have been put down by the brutal use of force, and successfully.

No, but if Caiphas had troubled to inform himself properly about our Lord's teaching, he would have realized that this new gospel had nothing to do with raising a revolution against the Romans, like those others. Rather, it was revolutionary in a new sense—it encouraged men to look out beyond death, and consider what would be the state of their souls at the Resurrection. The Resurrection—was that bluff? Caiphas was a Sadducee, and not much inclined to believe in it. But if you doubted it, you had only to go as far as Bethany, and contemplate the empty tomb of Lazarus. Caiphas was, I suspect, one of those people who are out to avoid disturbances and commotions at all costs; that is why he felt it necessary to liquidate the Nazarene. But in truth he ought to have paused, as modern men of science pause now and again, to reflect on the tremendous possibilities of those natural forces which they are letting loose. Caiphas was letting loose a world-revolution which has lasted from his day to ours; all to give another forty years' life to Jerusalem.

The man who thought he was playing for safety was playing with fire. If he had been a man of principle, jealous, albeit mistakenly jealous, for the honour of the Jewish people, he would have seen to it that our Lord was put to death by stoning. But Caiphas was not a man of principle; the charge of blasphemy did not really mean much to him; he was a statesman, only concerned to keep the Romans in a good temper. So our Lord must be handed over to the Romans for punishment, before his propaganda really became dangerous. For that reason, our Lord was crucified; and the picture of a Man hanging on a cross became part of the world's symbolism; has haunted, ever since, the imagination of mankind. Thousands of people, in the ancient world, suffered in that way; the mention of it was a familiar joke. But we do not fail to recognize the symbol; when we see the figure of a Man represented in that attitude, it does not occur to us to wonder whether it might be somebody else. The body is stripped; it is a pauper's death. The hands and feet are nailed, as if to express the fixity of a redemptive purpose. The arms are stretched out, in a gesture of welcome, and at the same time of intercession. The head is bowed in acquiescence. And the heart is wounded.

But indeed, the thing is simpler than that. The cross itself is a providentially appointed sign of contradiction, the very sign spoken of by Simeon in the temple. It cancels, it erases; bids us take no notice of what was there before, and start again. And that is symbolic of the fact that Chris-

tianity and the world are perpetually at cross-purposes. We
have no difficulty about seeing that in the large; we are conscious of it every time we open a newspaper. But don't let
us talk about the newspapers; the conflict, the contradiction
is there in every Christian heart; in your heart and mine. We
have been so familiar, all our lives, with that figure of the
cross and the condemned Man hanging on it; you would
think it had lost all power to move, or to impress us. But
no; ever so slightly, when we kneel in front of it, the crucifix raises a dumb protest which reverberates in our consciences.

There *is* enough of fallen nature in us to make us feel
uncomfortable, isn't there? There *is* a struggle between two
lives, the life of nature and the life of grace, going on within
us all the time; and we can't really make any accommoda-
tion between the two. We try to integrate them, but it
won't work; it is like trying to make your dream world fit
into the real world when you have just woken up from
sleep. Which is the dream world, which is the real world;
the life of nature, or the life of grace? Your crucifix gives
you the answer.

The artists, the sculptors of our day make symbolism so
difficult for us; we must dig so deep into the underworld of
our thought, before we can interpret their message. But
this figure of the Crucified is something standardized; so
many famous Madonnas in the world, but how many famous
Crucifixions?—and the message of it lies on the surface;
it is like a road-sign, making the situation clear to the mean-
est comprehension; no wayfaring man so foolish he can go
astray. You have only to look for a moment at those five

surface impressions we mentioned just now—impressions which might convey themselves, you would think, to a child or a savage looking at the crucifix for the first time—to see how each of them strikes a chord in the very depths of the human heart.

Jesus is stripped of his garments; this is the Man who told us, not long ago, that we ought not to fret over our body, how to keep it clothed; the God who clothed the grasses of the field would do as much and more for us. See here the result of his childlike improvidence; he hangs there naked. He told us, too, that if a man would take our cloak away from us, we should let him have our coat too; the world has taken him at his word, and he hangs there naked. And yet somehow we know better than to suppose that this is a casual instance of poetic justice; the connexion of thought lies deeper than that. Our Lord wanted to suffer stripped, precisely in order to remind us of those words of his, about stripping ourselves of worldly cares and worldly possessions.

Listen to what it says in the *Imitation of Christ*: "This must be your endeavour, this your prayer, this your preference, that you should manage to be stripped of all possessiveness, and follow in the footsteps of Jesus naked as he." And when the *Imitation of Christ* talks about being stripped of possessiveness, it doesn't just mean living simply on a small income; it means giving up all ambition, all desire for human praise, all greediness for any kind of comfort, spiritual consolations included. We ought to aim at that, it says; and if we can't bring ourselves to aim at it, we ought to pray that it may happen to us; and if we can't bring ourselves to utter that prayer, we ought at least to make it our preference—we should *like* to be people like that. Stripped, as if for a wrestling-match; no integuments of worldliness to give the devil a hand-hold.

And the great thing about that, of course, is honesty; absolute honesty with ourselves and with God. We have got to be stripped of those pretences by which we manage to build up such a fine picture of ourselves for the admiration of our friends, and even for our own. The motives which dictate our actions from day to day are very largely worldly ones; the crucifix does not dominate in our lives; it is only an occasional embarrassment. And it will be a long time before we strip ourselves of that worldliness; meanwhile, we can do something by stripping ourselves of those pretences which try to make out that the worldliness isn't there. The kind of worldliness, I mean, which prefers the more attractive duty to the less attractive; which makes us take more trouble about the people we want to stand well with; which allows us to secure our own comfort under the pretext of securing comfort for other people. And even that last rag which we cling to—the self-flattery which suggests to us that we are being rather humble when we tell our Lord that of course we aren't a bit like him; even that has to go, when we are really face to face with the Crucified.

Next, the atmosphere of the composition is one of tension; the body hangs from hands and feet with a sense of almost intolerable strain. If it be a carved crucifix you contemplate, that fact is conventionally represented in its very workmanship; the figure really does hang from the nails. If it be of ivory, so that the arms were carved out of the same piece as the body, they will be mortised to it, as if to emphasize the frailty of their support. We are told, I think, that the sculpture of classical Greece always represented the human figure in a gesture of repose. There is no repose about the crucifix, and for an excellent reason. Your classical statue, Mercury new-lighted on a heaven-kissing hill, or whatever it might be, reminded you that the pagan gods were part of nature, enclosed within its limits and incapable of rebellion against it. The Christian emblem represents tension; the perpetual state of tension there is between nature and grace. If the Author of nature, by becoming incarnate, has imprisoned himself within the framework of it, he is nevertheless in an attitude of perpetual conflict with a fallen world. He depends, but he does not rest on it. He hangs there, the victim of a divine discontent.

And for the Christian, as for Christ, there is no living in this fallen world without a sense of tension which never leaves him, simply because sin is there. "With Christ I hang upon the cross," St. Paul writes; and you find that about St. Paul. He visits Athens; does he stand spell-bound as he admires the splendid monuments of antiquity? No, "his heart was moved within him, to find the city so much given over to idolatry." The greatest of all the burdens he carries is his anxious care for all the churches; "Does anyone feel a scruple? I share it. Is anyone's conscience hurt? I am ablaze with indignation"—there is no rest for him anywhere, in a sin-world. So it is with all the saints; they mind sin. Not in that attitude of gleeful reprobation which we describe as "being shocked." No, to be shocked is to be

surprised; and they are not surprised to find the thoughts of
man set on evil. But they mind it; resent it as you or I would
resent an undeserved criticism passed on somebody we
loved. You and I, the non-saints, ought to share that feeling. Oh, we must judge other people with all possible
charity, make all possible allowances; but the existence of
evil around us ought to afflict us with a permanent sense of
malaise; we must never say, "I suppose people are like that."
And our own sins, our own sinfulness, ought to set up an
even greater sense of tension; we must never say, "I suppose
I am like that." No matter what morass of wickedness a man
may have fallen into, there is always hope for him as long
as he takes the strain of being a Christian.

Pain drives us in upon ourselves, and the attitudes into
which it forces us, or tries to force us, are those of self-pity.
Providentially, the form of martyrdom for which the policy
of Caiphas destined our Lord was one which forces from
the sufferer an attitude of world-awareness. An attitude of
welcome—how often we have seen in newspaper pictures,
if we have not seen it at first hand, the Holy Father wel-
coming the pilgrims who crowd about his path with that
magnificent open-armed gesture of his, all the better for
being quite unstudied, quite unconventional. St. John, com-
menting on Caiphas' dictum about one man dying for the
sake of the nation, points out that our Lord died "not only
for the nation's sake, but to bring together into one all God's
children, scattered far and wide." He will not beckon a soul
here, a soul there; if he is lifted up, it is so as to attract *all*
men to himself. And the gesture of welcome is also a gesture
of intercession. The Greeks, we are told, did not kneel

when they prayed; they stood with arms extended. A heathen visitor, coming suddenly upon the scene of Calvary, might have said, "I thought at first he was praying." Our Lord does not merely welcome us, with those open arms of his, he offers us up to the Father, associates us with his Sacrifice. All day long I have stretched out my hands; one o'clock sounds, two o'clock sounds, and our Lord is still praying.

And can we kneel in front of the crucifix without being ashamed of the narrow limits we set to our friendships, to our charity, the selectiveness of our prayers, the parochialism of our ambitions? Can we kneel in front of the crucifix without despising the half-heartedness, the perfunctoriness of our own devotions; our foolish habit of forgetting that when we pray we pray in him, and he prays in us?

In many representations of the crucifixion you will see our Lord's head bowed; either forwards or so as to rest on one shoulder. That he did bow his head at the moment of his death, St. John tells us; St. John, often the least graphic, but sometimes the most graphic, of our authorities. The other evangelists simply say that he yielded up his spirit, but they give us no evidence of it; what the watchers beneath the cross actually noticed was the bowed head which assured them that the struggle was over. It will have seemed, to some of them, a merely reflex action; not so, I think, to St. John. I think we are meant to see it as a deliberate gesture, not caused by, but accompanying and symbolizing, the act of death; a gesture of acquiescence. Our Lord does not bow to the inevitable; how could anything be inevitable to incarnate God? He bows, at a decreed moment, to the will of his heavenly Father. Those lips have spoken for the last time, but still he will communicate with us in sign-language. "Yes," says the bowed head, "yes, it *is* best that one man should be put to death, for the sake of the people."

It is when we contemplate that expression of acquiescence in him, who of his own will chose suffering, chose death, that we find out the secret of resignation; of bowing to the inevitable, not because it is inevitable, but because it is the will of God. We too will accept suffering, accept death, not with a fatalistic shrug of the shoulders, but with a voluntary adhesion to God's will thus expressed for us. His will is sacred; we shall not be content to *let* it happen; we shall *want* it to happen.

Sometimes the carver of our crucifix has been guilty of an anachronism. He means us to see our Lord still living and suffering on the cross, still teaching us by word or by gesture. But, as if determined to get in everything, he shows us the mark of the spear in the pierced side. And we are grateful to him for the anachronism; because, after all, that wound in the side is symbolic of something which does not belong to the order of time—the love of Jesus Christ for mankind, for you and me. He has borne all the martyrdom of his Passion so unflinchingly, so uncomplainingly—we were half afraid that his was the attitude of the Stoic, indifferent to all sentiment, contemptuous of all weakness in himself, or in others. His very sufferings proved him divine; but, was he human? And St. John once more reassures us; "this is he who came by water and by blood"—

the mixture of those two elements on Calvary is the symbol that attests the fact of a divine-human redeemer. So much else Calvary had to teach us; it was left for the spear of Longinus to lay open the treasures of a human heart.

And that lesson, Love claiming love, is the most important of all; is the link which unites, is the medium which sustains the rest. "I may have utter faith," St. Paul says, "so that I can move mountains; I may give away all that I have, to feed the poor; I may give myself up to be burnt at the stake; if I lack charity, it goes for nothing."

9 The Holy Rosary

THERE are two obvious objections to my talking to you about the holy rosary. The first is, you know the holy rosary so well that there's no need to think about it. And the other is, you've said the holy rosary so often that if the truth were told you've got tired of its monotonous repetitions, so you don't want to think about it. But isn't it possible that those two objections really cancel out? The reason why we get tired of saying the rosary so much, is because we think about it so little. We don't treat it exactly as if it were a prayer-wheel, but we treat it very much as if it were a prayer-wheel; we don't really want to say it, we want to get it said. And of course that can't be the right way to go about it.

What *is* the rosary? It's a curious thing, but if you consult various little pious books, you will find that there are three different ways of translating the prayer at the end of it. "That we, meditating on these mysteries—*with* the holy rosary," some books say, as if it were a kind of gadget, like a screw-driver. "On the holy rosary," other books say, as if it were a bus that would get you rapidly to your destination. But the other books give you "in the holy rosary"; and that I think is at once the most accurate and the most comforting translation of the three. Because you see the thing you call your rosary, the thing you carry about with you and break and lose, ought really to be called your rosary-beads; and so it would be if you lived in Ireland. But a rosary means a rose-garden. And the prayer at the Mass of October the 7th is really a very beautiful prayer, asking that we may benefit by meditating on the mysteries of our Lord's life, death and resurrection in the rose-garden of the Blessed Virgin Mary.

We might picture it, don't you think, as having more or less the shape of a shamrock; with the entrance where the stalk comes, and three circles of rose-bushes in front of us, white ones on the left, for the joyful mysteries, red straight in front of us, for the sorrowful; yellow to the right, for the glorious ones. Each circle has five separate rose-trees in it, and our Lady's face grows grave or lights up as she shows us one after another, for these are her memories. She will not let us pass through just sniffing the fragrance of them; she will bend down the branches and bring the flowers close to us, so that we can draw a deep breath and drink in the full flavour of the scent.

Or even, if you will, let us think of her as our mother, and ourselves as children; and she is teaching us a game which is centred on these fifteen rose-trees, the difficult and exciting game we call "life." She has to explain it over and over again, because we are so stupid and so inattentive; that is why it sometimes seems monotonous. Forgive me if I ask you to think of yourselves as children. But it's a curious thing that, the older you get, the more content you are to think of our Lady as your mother, understanding you, and yet not taken in by your pretences, knowing better than you do what is good for you, treasuring up your keepsakes for fear you should lose them. And the game—oh, the game is full of excitement. But at every turn of it, her shadow falls across the picture; she has played it, and played it so well.

What I'm suggesting is that we should run through that well-known, that all-too-well-known list of divine happenings, not exactly looking at them through her eyes, or thinking of them as relating to her; no, but with her beside us, pointing to the heart of each mystery and saying, "This is what it meant to me; what is it going to mean to you?"

With the Joyful Mysteries, it's easy to do that; it is all sunshine in her rose-garden, and she figures in each event. She figures; do not let us say she is the central figure—she is careful not to let us think that. Even at the Annunciation, what is important is not the honour done to her, but the work of grace which is being done in and through her. The story of Paradise is repeating itself, but with variations; God, who once made a woman miraculously out of a man, is now making a Man miraculously out of a woman; and woman, whose disobedience was once the preface to man's rebellion against God, now, by her obedience, prefaces the perfect sacrifice of God made Man. She shrinks away, not in fear, like Zachary, of an angel's visit, but in a kind of outraged humility that she should be thus saluted as "full of grace"; all through those years, so graciously lived, it had never occurred to her how full of grace she was. But she accepts the title; that grace was a gift, and a gift bestowed

on her in virtue of the miracle by which, here and now, a
Divine Life is being formed in her. And "You," she says,
"do you realize that when you were baptized, the same
thing happened to you—you became full of grace? No, do
not shrink from the title; it is there in black and white in
the sixth verse of St. Paul's epistle to the Ephesians. He
uses the same word; speaks of the grace with which they,
common or garden converts of his at Ephesus, have been
made full. Not in the same measure, because grace comes
to each of us in accordance with his or her capacity; but
your soul received, when you were baptized, all the grace
of which it is capable. Gratitude for that, humility over
that, that is the first step if your life is to be lived as mine
was."

And then, with the scent of this first mystery still in our
nostrils, just when we were beginning to think that religion
meant having everything done for you, that all you had got
to do was to lie back, and say "Yes, Lord, let it be unto me
according to thy word," she takes us on to the next rose-
bush, the Visitation. "Mary arose with haste and went into
the hill-country"; she didn't sit there meditating, she got up
and did something, did it before it was too late. (Do you
know how often that word "arise" comes in the Bible?
About a hundred and fifty times. I expect that was because
we aren't very good at arising. Because our Lady had become the Mother of God, she must put herself at the service
of her fellow-men.) And you (she says) must learn next
to co-operate with the grace freely given to you. You have
got to arise, and do something; with haste, do it now, or
you may miss the opportunity; and go into the hill-country,

do the difficult things, not just the easy ones; that is what grace is for.

When we come to the third mystery, our Lord's Birth, it hardly seems, does it, as if we had anything more to learn about that? We have contemplated it in the Crib, Christmas after Christmas—the splendid simplicity of it all! God come to earth, lying there in the half-darkness, with the champing of the oxen all round him, alone with the shepherds and the stars. Is there anything else you can add to the picture? Why, yes; we might remind ourselves that it was very cold. Simplicity is beautiful to contemplate, pleasant perhaps in retrospect, but at the time. . . . I don't mean that our Lady was worrying about herself; St. Joseph did that. But that he, her Son, should have no better welcome than this! Yes, be simple, she tells us, but be really simple; accept, not only for yourself but for those you love, the worst of things; then you will be like me.

The Presentation—there you have to throw yourself back into an Old Testament setting. "A son, her first-born"; because he was her first-born, he was forfeit to God. The first-born of a dumb beast must be offered in sacrifice; the first-born of a woman must be redeemed by the sacrifice of a dumb beast, to show that he belonged to God, not to his parents. By that act, he could redeem his younger brothers and sisters; the first-born did duty for the whole family. So our Lord came, St. Paul tells us, to be the first-born of many brethren; to redeem us by his sacrifice. He was all the child our Lady had, and he belonged to God, not to her. And you, she tells us, belong to God, not to yourselves. When

you put self first, you refuse God his rights. You are to
live for God.

And that may mean the loss of all we thought made life
worth living; bitter separations, cruel relinquishments. She
had a foretaste of that in the fifth of her still joyful
mysteries, she had lost our Lord and found him again, only
to be told that he belonged to God, not to her. As we
leave the first circle of her rose-garden, the sun goes in;
there is twilight about us. Only that means—Chesterton
notices it somewhere—that colours stand out brighter. The
red roses are more beautiful in the shade.

Sometimes, when we are saying the rosary, we wonder
why this or that "mystery" should have been called a
mystery at all—but not when it comes to the Agony in the
Garden; that is mystery through and through. We see our
Lord prostrated by grief over the treachery of his friend,
the ingratitude of his fellow-countrymen; see him the victim
of that nervous shrinking which makes us recoil from the
thought of death; and we can only tell ourselves that he had
all our human weaknesses, sin only excepted. We wonder
why he should give way publicly to these apprehensions,
parade them, almost; and we can only tell ourselves that he
wanted us to know the human side of him through and
through. If you come to think of it, there is a third subject
for surprise—how did *we* come to know of it? He was
alone there under the olive trees; his enemies had not
reached the scene yet, his friends were asleep. Our Lord,
then, must have described it to somebody after the resurrection; to whom? Only St. Luke tells us about the sweat of

blood; only St. Luke tells us about the angel who came to comfort the Son of God in his distress; and St. Luke, according to tradition, was the confidant of the Blessed Virgin. Gethsemani, for her, is not a first-hand memory, but she, I think, was responsible for handing the story down to us. It may come to you, she warns us, treachery on the part of those you love, ingratitude, despondency, the fear of death. All these may assail you, but they must not embitter you; may cast you down, but they must leave your will true to the will of God.

The Scourging—no likelihood that she was there to witness that. But she will have read the story of it in the piteous traces it had left; all that disfigurement of the body that had come from her. On that scene, I think, she does not dwell; but she warns us that it has a meaning in our lives. You, too, she says, will encounter bodily suffering, much of it perhaps. May it be yours to bear it as he bore it, undeserved by your own self-indulgence, in proof of your patience and your love, in part-expiation of the world's guilt.

She may, perhaps, have stood there among the crowd when the doors of the praetorium opened, and her Son was led out by the soldiers, dressed up in a property robe of state, with a trail of bramble wound about his head, to look like a crown. "See," says Pilate, "here is the Man!" It takes our breath away, because we feel the tragic irony of it. But at the time—what did it sound like at the time? "Here the fellow is," says Pilate; "look at him!" Not, I think, in mere mockery; it is clear from all our accounts of the Passion that Pilate really wanted an acquittal. He is playing his last card, by representing our Lord to the crowd as a madman; he

dressed him up as a kind of Guy Fawkes, to make the Jews
feel the absurdity of it all. And they, I think, laughed, but
laughed without good humour; a shout of laughter went up
from the crowd, and she heard it. Perhaps, in a way, that
was her worst moment; nothing is more contrary to our
nature than to bear contempt. And that is what she tells us
to do, when we recite the third Sorrowful Mystery; you
have got to resign yourself to looking a fool, being thought
a fool, even being a fool, when it is God's will that you
should make this sacrifice to him. Some of the saints have
gone out of their way to cultivate it; St. Philip Neri, for
example. But how hard it is!

Tradition will have it, though without any support from
Scripture, that our Lady met her Son on the way to Calvary;
it seems likely enough. If so, what she will have noticed
above all will have been his intense physical weariness; her
mother's instinct would fasten on that. And she tells us to
be ready for that, too; to be ready with heroic efforts of endurance, when duty or charity demands them of us—to go
on and on giving our best, and never advertise what we are
doing by boastful complaints.

So far, these sorrowful memories of hers have been
memories at second hand; or at least of something seen
momentarily, felt with a single stab. But on Calvary we
know that she was there, and we have no reason to doubt
that she was there the whole time. She will have heard the
cry, "My God, my God, why hast thou forsaken me?"—
heard it, and wondered, but without ever ceasing to believe. Hitherto he has never been the victim of his moods,
this Son of hers; he has wept, and been angry, and shown

amazement, but always he has been perfectly master of himself. Now, his sufferings have penetrated to the very fortress of his soul; and she warns us that we too must be prepared for the extreme of nervous fatigue; for times when God seems distant and prayer seems useless, when we are left in the dark, and alone. And beyond all that, for the darkness and loneliness of death. May she be with us then.

And then suddenly, as we turn the corner into the third circle of mysteries, the sun comes out again, brighter than ever, and our Lady's memories are all of gracious things. Why are we not told, in the gospels, about the circumstances in which she first met her risen Son? I think because the gospels are out to give us sensational evidence of the resurrection—how our Lord appeared to the Magdalen just when she had given up all hope, to Thomas when he refused to believe; his appearance to his Blessed Mother wasn't news, because she had believed all along. But there is no meeting which the mind dwells on more contentedly than that of the Virgin Mother with her Son, just risen from the virgin tomb; it is full of the fresh, clean airs of spring-tide, everything is made new. And, "See," she tells us, "what it means, the forgiveness of your sins! They are dead, like last year's leaves, and you have risen to new life, with all that put behind you."

But that reunion, we reflect, what a short time it lasted! Only forty days, and then she must learn to do without him again; live the rest of her life as a childless widow. But no, we are wasting our pity on her. She had faced all that difficulty, at the time when she lost him and found him in the temple; "Could you not tell," he asked, "that I must be in the place which belongs to my Father?" His words were beyond her understanding at the time; but she has thought them over and mastered them. Of course he has gone back to the place which is his Father's, to heaven; for her, as for us, this world is a place of probation; she must prove her faith and her love by believing in him, loving him, in absence. And she warns us that we are not to expect the service of Christ in this world to be all plain sailing; there will be dull, flat times when we seem to get nothing out of our religion, and it is all an uphill job. It is then, she says, that we shall be able to prove our faith and love; when he seems to be taken from us, and a cloud hides him from our sight.

In what strength are we to do that? In the same strength which she and the holy apostles received on the day of Pentecost. Once more, as at Nazareth, the Holy Spirit came upon her, and the power of the most High overshadowed her; and Christ was born anew, this time in his mystical Body, the Church. And you, she says, living with the life of that Body, are in the full stream of the Holy Spirit's influence. Deep down in you, too deep for your discovery, lies the same power that set all Jerusalem astir, on the day when the Church was born. Strike out, and do something for God; you are stronger than you know.

But all the years she lived—we do not know how many— after her Son's Ascension, there was a bond of love that still bound them together, cords of the second Adam which moored her heart in heaven. Until at last it seemed as if that attachment were too strong; earth could not detain her, and she slipped away from us, leaving us never a tomb to venerate, never a relic to kiss: she must be all his. That is what the Assumption means; and she bids us keep that in our thoughts, make that our dream, to be so one with Christ that life on earth seems only an episode, death only the surmounting of an obstacle. Do not tell me that we are very far from feeling like that; we cannot feel like that, but we shall be poor Christians if we do not wish that we could.

Nearly over now; only one more decade—faint hearts that we are, we are still longing to get finished. But the end, they say, crowns the work; and our crown, in the last resort, will be fashioned of no other material than the crowns the saints wear, the crown our Lady wears in eternity; moments of time dedicated to Jesus Christ. May we so meditate on these mysteries in the rose-garden of the Blessed Virgin Mary, that we may imitate what they contain, and attain what they promise.

IO The Holy Eucharist

WE WILL single out one or two of the gracious character-
istics which marked our Lord's life on earth, and see how
they are reflected, in a kind of mystical light, by the manner in which he comes to us in Communion. And perhaps
just by the way, just in passing, we will take a look at our
own lives and ask whether these same gracious character-
istics are reflected there quite as much as they ought to be.

When St. Paul wrote his second letter to the Corinth-
ians, he was writing to people who had really wounded
him; the criticisms they passed on him had really got in
under his skin. And the appeal he makes to them at the beginning of his tenth chapter, where he starts to unmask
his guns, is: "I beseech you therefore, brethren, by the
courtesy of Christ." I love that phrase, "the courtesy of
Christ"; such a vivid phrase that it would have taken St.
Paul to think of it. (The translators all miss it, except Mof-
fat, who has "consideration"—he means, "considerateness.") We are so accustomed to think of our Lord's life
written in large, the great broad outlines of it, his devotion
to his Father's will, his generosity, his fearless courage, that
we miss, if we are not careful, the details. We ought, now
and again, to bend down and see the grasses, as it were,

between the stems of the forest; and I think if we do that
one of the first qualities we shall notice in our Blessed Lord
is his courtesy, his considerateness for all the different
people he had to deal with. That is the quality I want to
emphasize in this meditation. I want you to see him as, on
the merely human side, always thoughtful and therefore
always lovable.

The first mark of his courtesy we will discuss is his unobtrusiveness. And when I use that word, I am not speaking of the hidden life which he took upon himself merely
by the circumstances of his Incarnation. Isaias had spoken
of Almighty God as a God who hides himself; the God
who made heaven and earth, who gives us life with all its
rich experience and colour, and leaves it at our doors as a
kind of mysterious present from the Father whom we
never see. And our Blessed Lord, as we know, would imitate his heavenly Father; he would be a Christ who hides
himself. The stable at midnight, the long years of obscu-
rity at Nazareth, the ignominy of his Passion—all these are
things we have often meditated upon, and admired the
great humility in which he came to us. But it is something
else I wanted to speak of just now, the unobtrusiveness
with which he approached the men of his age. You will
remember how St. Matthew, in describing his ministry,
recalls the quotation "He will not protest and cry out;
none shall hear his voice in the streets." He came with a
mission, the greatest mission of all time; and you expect to
find a missionary—how should we blame him for it?—
going about in such a way as to court public attention.
Instead of that, you will find that after his first sermon in

the synagogue at Nazareth our Lord never makes any attempt to bring himself into notice—it is all the other way.

All the time, people are thronging round him, and all the time he is trying to escape from them, steals off to the mountain-side, or gives them the slip by unexpectedly sailing across the Lake of Galilee. Not once but commonly his miracles are accompanied by an urgent command that nothing must be said about it. He does not stand at the street corners to get a crowd, does not make his way into palaces, and tax Herod with his incontinence, the Romans with their oppression. If he talks to anybody uninvited, it will be a poor cripple sitting by a pool, a widow carrying out her only son to burial. For the rest, if you want him you must go to look for him; he will not force his company on you. He will take people as they come.

The Holy Eucharist is a memorial of our Lord's death; it is also a memorial of his life. And in particular—the thing hardly needs to be said—it recalls to us that unobtrusiveness of which we have been speaking. It is *we* that gild the ciborium and house it in silk; nothing is to be seen there except common bread; it is under that guise that he will conceal his presence. Even when we receive him in Communion, our faith must go out to meet him; he will give no sign to tell us who it is that comes to us, how it is that he comes to us. Easy to pass him by without reverence, easy to forget about him. He is just there if he is wanted; that is all.

The modern world is no place for unobtrusiveness, and we should not be too ready to criticize our neighbours if they seem, in their public capacity, to love the limelight.

They have a message, it may be, for the world, and they can see no other way of delivering it. But it may be worth while to glance for a moment at our own lives, and ask whether we are imitating, in this particular, the courtesy of Jesus Christ. To be always up in arms, always airing your opinions for the benefit of an audience which disagrees, and may be provoked by them, or of an audience which agrees, and may be bored by them; to insist that all your friends *must* read such and such a book, *must* go to hear such and such a preacher; to be continually offering your advice, continually taking duties upon yourself because the other person is certain to make a hash of them—all this is not to be guilty of any great imperfection. But you have not, to that extent, shown forth the image of Jesus Christ.

He was there when he was wanted; he was always there whenever he was wanted. Only for a few hours could he escape, would he escape, from the throng of his suppliants. No impression stands out more clearly, I think, from the very short record which the gospels give us, than this; he was hardly ever alone. If he shunned publicity, he did not indulge his taste for privacy. He was for all alike; the publican and the sinner could find access to him, and he would not shut out the malignant faces of his enemies, there at the edge of the crowd, taking notes. He wouldn't get rid of people; wouldn't get rid of the Syrophenician woman, when his disciples implored him to, because she was being such a nuisance. "Send her away"—that means, I fancy, "Do what she asks; we shall never get rid of her otherwise." But our Lord wasn't going to spare himself the trouble of an interview by doing a miracle, so to speak, over his shoulder; he was too courteous.

He was for everybody; and now, in the Holy Eucharist, he is for everybody still. What a thought-provoking thing it is to stand in some big church on a Sunday morning and see the communicants, row after row of them, streaming up to the altar rails. Here is a cross-section of humanity, more complete than any you could find elsewhere. Usually, if you see a crowd of people all making in the same direction, there is some special interest that claims them—they are all that kind of people. But here are men, women and children, all sorts, educated and uneducated, serious and frivolous, feeble and healthy, all wanting the same thing. Usually we have to pay for anything that is worth having, and one particular set of incomes crowd in at one particular door; but here are rich and poor alike, there is no discrimination, no chance of anybody being turned away. Usually, among a crowd of people, there is some sort of crowd spirit; here, each is a lonely individual, yet they are all going the same way.

And how much more impressive it would be, if we could look into their hearts! There are all sorts here; perhaps there are some souls very near to God, saints almost; only you cannot tell them from the others. There are daily communicants, who are not saints or anything like it: what a world of imperfections, in spite of all that piety! There are people who come regularly, once a week, once a fortnight; some, not all, have made great sacrifices to go as often as that; some, not all, wish they could go oftener. There are people who only go now and again, when the mood takes them; some go very seldom, but a birthday or an anniversary has brought them this morning. And there may be some—God forbid that it should be so—who have not cleansed their consciences of mortal sin, and yet, from human respect, or because they have judged their motives too lightly, are going to receive Communion with the rest. And all alike are to receive the same thing, the Body, Soul and Divinity of our Lord Jesus Christ.

Our Lord, when he was on earth as Man, would preach even to his enemies; they would get no good out of it, nay, they would redouble their guilt by taking advantage of his words to defame him, but he would not send them away, he would leave them their free will. So, when he comes to earth in the Holy Eucharist, he leaves men their free will; to some of them the divine gift will be useless, and worse than useless. But even among the rough-and-tumble of the crowds who listened to our Lord, what a lot of half-hearted disciples there must have been! Would he not have done better to gather round him a little nucleus of really faithful souls? But no, he had something for everybody; a hundredfold, sixtyfold, thirtyfold—in most of them the sowing of the Word would produce a poor crop, but it was something. So it is with the Holy Eucharist; you would think it would have been jealously reserved for a handful of saints, a gift so holy, so awe-inspiring as this! But no, it is for the rough-and-tumble of us as well; ours will be a poor harvesting, but he will reap what he can.

Shall we have the courage, once again, to take a glance at our own lives, and see how they reflect the splendid impartiality of our Divine Redeemer? *He* didn't spend all his time talking to our Lady and to his apostles. Oh, to be sure, there will always be those who have a first claim upon us, our family, our friends, our immediate neighbours. God means us to find ourselves in a particular setting, and it would be wrong to neglect these claims by giving ourselves out too freely to all comers. But isn't it true, with most of us, that we like to keep as far as possible to our own small circle, seize upon every excuse for turning our backs on the intrusive stranger—"After all, what claim has So-and-so on me"? Especially the people we don't get on with, the bores, the exacting people, those who don't seem to appreciate us? I know; but what claim had they on our Lord, those exacting multitudes who followed him? How many of them, do you suppose, really appreciated him? As we come away from Communion, disheartened as usual by the little fruit it seems to bear in our lives, let us remember sometimes that Christ, the Christ whom it is our duty to imitate, was too courteous to turn us, even us, away.

But this courtesy of his goes further yet; although he is dealing, all his life, with crowds, he will never deal with them as crowds, but as individuals. Do you remember the story of the woman with an issue of blood? She came up to him when he was in a hurry, on his way to heal the daughter of Jairus; came up to him in the middle of a crowd, so that she managed to touch the hem of his garment, without being seen by anybody; and immediately she was cured. Our Lord asks "Who touched me?", and when St. Peter points out that it might have been some casual contact, he insists on having an answer; a healing virtue has gone out of him, and he knows it; where is the *miraculée*? Why was he so specially keen to interview her? I think because it was not part of his programme to glorify God with mass-produced miracles; each person he cured must be brought into personal relations with him, must be able to say afterwards, "He turned, and spoke to me." Of all those thousands who lay on their pallets by the roadside, not one was healed but carried away some memory of his voice; "Go, and sin no more," "Thy faith has saved thee"; it was to be a personal experience.

They are not just faces in a crowd; they are all real people to him. How easily he distinguishes between the merely curious and the genuine enquirer! "I will follow thee wherever thou art going"—here is a man who is inquisitive to know where the prophet lives; "Foxes have holes," he is told, "and the birds of the air their resting-places; the Son of Man has nowhere to lay his head." And yet, when the two friends ask, "Rabbi, where dost thou live?" he will entertain them till sundown. How he distinguishes between the self-assured and the humble approach! The gentleman from Herod's court, who is so insistent, "Sir, come down before my child dies," must be content with the promise, "Thy son is to live"; the Roman sergeant, so well disciplined in obedience, is a different matter; "I will come and heal him."

How surely he recognizes, how gently he inspires, contrition, and at various levels! The woman of Samaria, with her pious platitudes, must be suddenly knocked off her perch with the command, "Go home, fetch thy husband." The woman taken in adultery is to be won by sympathy; "I

will not condemn thee either. Go, and do not sin again
henceforward." The Magdalen—she is pardoned already;
"If great sins have been forgiven her, she has also greatly
loved." How nicely graded are the demands he makes on
different souls! The young man who has kept all the commandments from his youth up must be sent home to sell
all that he has. But when poor Zacchaeus, the publican, has
been beckoned down from his eyrie in the sycamore-tree,
and announces, "I give half of what I have to the poor,"
that is enough; "He, too, is a son of Abraham." How well
he knows where faith is strong enough, where it is not yet
strong enough, to do without reassurance! The Magdalen
is to keep her distance; only Thomas may thrust his hand
into the wounds. Everybody, to our Lord, from our Blessed
Lady downwards, is a separate problem, needing a separate
approach.

And so it is, if only we had faith to believe it, in Holy
Communion. That long procession to the altar-rails, how
interminable it seems! The priest, you would think, must
get tired of muttering the same formula two or three hundred times over! But no, he is not allowed to say "Corpus
Domini nostri Jesu Christi custodiat *animas vestras*"; the
sacred words must be said to each communicant individually. Jesus Christ is not simply coming among us, he is
coming to each of us; and although the gift is always the
same (for it is nothing less than the whole of himself), the
purpose for which it is given, the influence which it is
meant to bestow, on your soul or mine, is something special,
in proportion to the needs of each, in accordance with the
plan he has for each. He knows you, and makes allowances

for you; knows you, and can gauge your capacity; knows you, and is not to be put off by excuses. He can tell whether you are really trying to find *him* when you go to the altar, or merely following the dictates of convention; whether you come in a spirit of humility, or expecting too much of him. He can tell whether the contrition you feel for your sins needs to be drawn out still more, or is ripening already into love; whether you are capable of great sacrifices or only of little ones; whether your faith is such that it still needs reassurance, or whether it can stand up to the test of a rebuff.

And I think there's a kind of moral for us, here too, to end up with. We said that we would try to imitate the courtesy of our Lord Jesus Christ by being for everybody; by throwing our sympathies open to everybody we met, instead of shutting ourselves up in a clique of people who happened to agree with us, happened to amuse us. And at first sight it might look as if that meant getting mixed up in all sorts of movements and agitations, going to committee meetings and passing resolutions, and signing letters to the newspapers. Well, I expect a lot of good is done that way, and we can have a lot of respect for the people who go in for that sort of thing, as long as it isn't mere love of interference. But if there is any truth in what we were saying about our Lord just now, this kind of mass-produced friendliness towards our fellow-men isn't all that is required of us, if we are to be like him. We have got to take a personal interest in people as people, try and get to know them and understand them and be some help, or at least some comfort to them.

Queen Victoria is said to have complained that Mr. Gladstone always addressed her as if she were a public meeting; and it's perfectly possible, without realizing it, to go through the world always trying to impose your personality on others, always airing your opinions and expecting them to be agreed with, never hearing what other people think at all. If you look at our Lord's conversations in the gospels, you will find that he nearly always starts them with a question. He never needed to ask questions; he knew what was in man. But he liked to draw people out, to hear what they had to say for themselves. I wonder if we, some of us, couldn't afford to do that a bit more?

And of course it's especially important for those who are entrusted with the education of others, for parents and school-teachers. Not to be always trying to impose your own pattern, to turn out a whole crowd of people on your own formula, but to study people's natures, people's aptitudes, help them to develop on their own lines. Oh, we shall often make a mess of it, to be sure; we can't read hearts as our Lord could. But we shall be better mirrors of his divine courtesy if we try, not just to be for all the people we meet, but for each person we meet; mirrors of that Divine Master who gives himself every morning to you, and you, and you.

HOLY HOUR
EARTHLY PARADISE
(i)

Our Lord said to the Penitent Thief, "This day thou shalt be with me in Paradise." From that scene of injustice, that arena of pain, those crowding faces, that exhausting experience, he is to be ushered, all in a moment, into inviolable repose. We ought to hear those same comforting words said to us when our Lord bids us leave, though it be only for a little, only for a short hour, the janglings of daily life and of common duty; invites us to be with him, his Eucharistic presence, in that sacred enclosure of which his tabernacle makes a paradise.

Let us imagine ourselves, then, in Paradise; not in that heavenly Paradise which is the reward of faithful souls; those joys cannot enter into mortal minds; let us imagine ourselves in that earthly Paradise which our first parents were created to inherit. What was the first activity that exercised the mind of Adam, when he opened his eyes to the world God had made for him?

Surely he found himself in that very attitude which is to be the first attitude of our minds during this Eucharistic Hour; ADORATION. To him, adoration must have been a spontaneous instinct; for us, lying under the curse, it is not so—we must go to creatures first, and find God in them. Adam's soul, in its primal innocency, will have gone straight to God, to the Author of gifts, rather than the gifts themselves; his mind will have gone out towards the thought of God before it even found leisure to turn back on itself. As the new-born child turns towards its mother, his soul will have turned towards the hand that had but now fashioned it—God, the source of all life and all being; how great, how wonderful, how worthy to be praised! That first act of human consciousness interpreted all the dumb praise of those other, earlier-born creatures, light and earth and waters, sun, moon, and stars, plants, fishes, birds and beasts; their praise found an expression at last. The first man was the priest of creation.

We have souls of our own to save, let us forget about that now. Let our first aspirations be away from self, away from creatures, directed towards God only. Here is our Lord present in his sacrament; let us adore God, as the canon of the Mass bids us, *per ipsum et cum ipso et in ipso*, "by him and with him and in him." *Per ipsum*—it is his spirit, breathed upon us from that tabernacle, that will make our dumb hearts vocal with praise. *Cum ipso*, our adoration will be acceptable, because it will be united here with the perpetual stream of adoration which goes up to the Father from the Heart of Jesus in the Eucharist. *In ipso*, for God is in Christ, reconciling the world to himself, and Christ is in the Sacred Host.

Adoration does, in fact, involve a comparison of ourselves with God—our infinite helplessness and worthlessness as creatures with his sufficiency, our Nothing with his All. But the more unconsciously that comparison is made, the better; you cannot despise yourself more thoroughly than by forgetting yourself altogether. Just for this first interval, then, of our Eucharistic hour, let us try to empty our minds of everything except the thought of God's Majesty, as we apprehend it in and through the tabernacle; let us fight off every thought which occurs to our minds except the thought of God, even ourselves, even our sins; let us allow the Holy Spirit to draw us out of ourselves and plunge us in adoration at our Lord's feet. Let us pierce beyond the veils of the Eucharistic species to the Sacred Humanity, and beyond the Sacred Humanity itself to the Divinity which is inseparable from it, till the centre of our hearts rests in the centre of all existence, God.

We won't think about our needs yet, we won't think about our sins yet, we won't think even about God's mercies yet; all that shall come later on. We will think simply about God, about his majesty, his holiness; or rather, we will not think about it, in the sense of conjuring up to our minds any theological considerations, in the sense of distracting our imaginations by calling up any mental image of him, conceiving his presence as if it were localized somewhere up in the air, or even referring our thoughts about him particularly to the tabernacle. We will simply leave our minds open in an attitude of loving attention towards him, leaving him to do the rest, confining our own efforts to beating back, quietly, as they come, the distractions which try to fill our minds and overcloud them with a mist of worldly imaginations. Just for ten minutes, we will be content to hold ourselves at God's disposal; free for God.

(ii)

When Adam first looked away from God, the regard of his mind fell upon himself, and upon the creation of which he was a part. All had been pronounced by its Creator to be very good. To us, even the face of God's creation is marred, because it reflects our own passions to us, our own sins; in the state of innocency, man was at peace with himself, at peace therefore with the world around him. Only one thing was needed—it was not good for man to be alone; he must see his own happiness mirrored in another pair of human eyes. So Eve was created to be a helpmeet for him; and now nothing could meet his eye, or present itself to his thoughts, which was not matter for THANKSGIVING. So he turned back to God, having learned, now, a new attitude of worship, that of thanksgiving for the blessings which surrounded him. And that attitude of thanksgiving is the second phase of our Eucharistic devotion; an essential one, for thanksgiving is the very meaning of the word "eucharist."

Let us, then, imitate him by turning back our eyes from the contemplation of God as he is in himself, and consider his goodness as he reveals it to us in the gift of his creatures. Let us still forget our sins, and the sins which disfigure the world around us; let us try to look out upon creation as if with those innocent, wondering eyes with which our first parents saw it. But not in detail, not giving any play to our discursive imagination. For God's creatures have this power over us, which they never had over our first parents before the Fall, of enchaining our imagination and preventing our minds from turning back to God. That is especially true of our pleasures and creature comforts. We must not waste this quarter of the Eucharistic hour by idle daydreams, by renewing our pleasures in memory. All we need is a general glance at the blessings with which God surrounds us, health and strength and appetite, friendships and interests and relaxations; it is enough to think of them in the gross. All the more so, because we have material for thankfulness to Almighty God which Adam never had.

More than for his natural benefits to us, we have to thank God for his benefits to us in the supernatural order; for the Incarnation, the Life, and the Death of his Son, with all the graces that spring from them. In that first Paradise there stood one tree whose fruit man was forbidden to eat; and punishment was threatened if this law were transgressed; "in the day when thou shalt eat of it thou shalt surely die." Under the new Dispensation, the Tree of the Cross has borne fruit for us in the Blessed Sacrament, and a different law prevails, Take and eat. The threat has been turned into a promise, "He that eateth of this Bread shall live for ever." *Per ipsum*—the chief cause of all our gratitude is our Lord himself, his Presence in the Eucharist; *cum ipso*, we unite our gratitude to his, when he thanked his Father for hiding his mysteries from the wise and prudent, and revealing them to babes; *in ipso*, once more we shall pierce through the veil, and find the Author of all these benefits face to face with us.

For that, then, first, and for his other benefits in the supernatural order. But let us give thanks for common blessings, too, in these next ten minutes; it is so valuable a habit to get into, and so rare. We think of a child as terribly rude if it does not say Thank you when we pass something across the table, but how do we treat Almighty God? What is the proportion between the prayers that go up for a fine day and the thanksgivings that go up when a fine day comes?

The root of all that trouble is our want of simplicity. We do need so much more of the spirit of St. Francis. We shall never learn to be properly grateful for God's gifts until we learn, like St. Francis, to treat them all as surprise gifts—to regard the sun when it rises as a kind of birthday present, the shade of the trees as a treat specially arranged for our benefit. We *will* take our blessings for granted, because we have never had to do without them. Ten lepers were sent to show themselves to the priest, and went away cleansed, but only one of them returned to give glory to God, and he was a despised Samaritan. *Gratias agamus Domino Deo nostro;* earth and sea and sky, and the Church militant, expectant and triumphant, respond, *Dignum et justum est.*

(iii)

We have been imagining ourselves in the earthly Paradise; but we are not really in that Paradise, though God is as close to us here as when he walked in his garden in the evening air. But sin has come in between us; as Adam and his wife would have hidden themselves from God's Presence, so we cannot come into God's Presence like this without being reminded of human sin. Our third attitude must be one of REPARATION.

When Adam had sinned, and been exiled from Paradise, there was nothing left for him but to spend the rest of his life in making reparation for his fault. And not for his fault only, but for all those sins of his descendants which would owe their origin to that primal disobedience; both as their forefather and as the cause of their guilt, he must needs make reparation for them too. Satisfaction he could not

make, because he had offended the infinite dignity of God.
But he could accept his punishment—the ground was to
bring forth thorns and briers to spoil his tilling, and he was
to eat bread in the sweat of his brow; in associating himself
with the justice of that punishment, he made what reparation he could. Satisfaction was not made, until the second
Adam came to us; and wore those thorns and briers as a
royal crown about his head, and atoned for our sins in the
garden of Gethsemani, by the sweat of his brow. In the
sweat of his brow he laboured to redeem us, laboured to
win Bread for us, that Bread of Life in which we here
adore his Presence. With all the benefits of Calvary to engage our gratitude, with all the merits of Calvary to shield
us from harm, we have offended and offend still. And, what
is worse, God's benefits are made the occasion for doing him
fresh injury. His presence in the Blessed Sacrament is profaned by carelessness, by irreverence, by indifference, by
slovenly Communions; worst of all, by deliberate outrage.
For such profanations above all we make reparation here,
we make reparation today. *Per ipsum*—the loving means by
which our Lord seeks to wean us away from sin has become
the cause of fresh sin in its turn. *Cum ipso*—we have no
victim with which to make our peace except this same Sacrament which we have defiled. *In ipso*—the Judge before
whom we must make amends awaits us in audience, here
on his Sacramental Throne. The Christian body is and
should be a solidarity throughout the world, and blas-
phemies or profanations committed even in the remotest
parts of the world should affect us as much as if they had
happened in our own country, under our own eyes.

Only, we shall do well to think of God's honour, to make reparation to God's honour, as it is injured by the people we live with, by the people who are our friends. In that connexion, there is one very obvious point we shouldn't lose sight of—all the devotions to the Blessed Sacrament which you will find in our modern English prayer-books are in fact foreign devotions; many of them are simply translated, others were composed under the influence of foreign models. Indeed, it is probably true that in the first days in which Christians were invited to make reparation to our Lord in his sacramental presence, that devotion was in the main intended to be a counterblast to the horrible ceremonies of black magic which used to be performed, were supposed, anyhow, to be performed, by the degenerates of seventeenth-century France. And when we are told to make reparation for actual outrage offered to our Lord in his sacramental presence we sometimes wonder whether, after all, this has very much to do with us. Does it very often happen, here and now, that the Blessed Sacrament is deliberately profaned?

Thank God, I believe it to be extremely uncommon. Such deliberate profanation demands a psychology which is not ours, a sort of borderland or twilight between faith and unbelief which makes it possible to go on hating God when you have ceased to fear him. I should suppose that even sacrilegious Communions are far less common in our own country than elsewhere. But I think we can still feel called upon to offer reparation for the *neglect* with which our Lord is treated among us; partly by those whose faith is untroubled, who make so little effort to communicate either frequently or worthily; partly by those who have begun to feel the pinch of religious difficulties, and immediately run away from the sacraments, dropping their arms without striking a blow. Let us remind ourselves that there are gaps at our side always, terrible gaps, when we worship, and let us offer our Lord reparation for the little trouble these people take about him. Any priest knows something of what the prayer of Gethsemani meant; it does not need a great stretch of the imagination for a layman to be able to appreciate it equally. We will unite our penitential tears, the sweat of our shame, with the agony our Lord underwent in the garden for our sins and the sins of the whole world.

(iv)

Man in the state of innocence may have prayed for the satisfaction of his needs, temporal and spiritual, but if so, it was only in recognition of his dependence; for his needs were satisfied by God's Providence not, indeed, as a matter of right, but as a matter of course. Since the Fall, man has been praying quite otherwise; has battered despairingly against the shut gates of Paradise. In a thousand tongues, under a thousand strange forms of idolatrous ritual, he has prayed for a successful harvest, victory over his enemies, and whatever else his soul craved. It is right that we should pray for what we need, it is a gracious act to pray even for what we covet; few of us could afford to omit the practice without danger of spiritual pride.

Most of us, even when we pray for others, are apt to be perhaps a little selfish in our PETITIONS, thinking more of those immediately around us, those who endear themselves to us, than of those whose need is greatest, those whose claim on us is in fact strongest. It was given to Adam, if he did but pray for his children and his children's children, to pray for the whole human race. And the second Adam, as he knelt in Gethsemani, prayed for the whole human race too; even for those who persecuted him, even for those who would, he knew, refuse the grace offered to them and frustrate the aim of his prayer. There is a model for us to set before us. . . . We tire so easily of praying for the soul that has drifted away from religion, for the apparently incorrigible sinner; our Lord prayed, even for those whose eternal damnation he foresaw. We have a perfect right to pray specially for those who have asked our prayers; but they must not monopolize them. As soon as we have made our special intention at Mass, we have to pray, too, for all whose faith and devotion is known to God. And I think we shall do well, even in our private prayers, when we intercede for one who is sick, to remember all the sick persons in the world; when we intercede for the sinner, to remember those souls throughout the world who are in danger of an impenitent death, and so on.

Here at least, where we are called apart to watch for an hour with our Master, let us fling our petitions as wide as possible. Let us pray for God's will to be done in and for every human creature. And especially, kneeling before the tabernacle, let us pray for the furtherance of our Lord's Eucharistic kingdom; for more Communions, not only in this parish or that, not only in our own country, but all over the world; more faithful Communions, more careful preparation, more fruitful thanksgiving. *Per ipsum*—the Eucharistic Presence is the weapon by which he will subdue the world to himself. *Cum ipso*—it is his own advocacy that we must plead for the attainment of that end. *In ipso*—the Author of all gifts, Almighty God, is here.

At the same time, let us not forget to pray for ourselves, who have shared this hour of watching with our Lord. Let us pray for the gift of perseverance, not trusting overmuch to the sentiments of loyalty and devotion which we experience upon such an occasion as the present; of the Twelve Apostles, there was only one who greeted his Master with a kiss in Gethsemani, and that one betrayed him. Let us pray for more recollection in the moments just before and just after Mass; those moments which are so vital to our spirituality, those moments which are so liable to disturbance and distraction. Let us pray for more love, more eagerness, more tenderness in our Communions. Even so, come, Lord Jesus, into our hearts.

I I The New Law

And I tell you that if your justice does not give fuller measure than the justice of the scribes and the Pharisees, you shall not enter into the kingdom of heaven. You have heard that it was said to the men of old, Thou shalt do no murder; if a man commits murder, he must answer for it before the court of justice. But I tell you that any man who is angry with his brother must answer for it before the court of justice, and any man who says Raca to his brother must answer for it before the Council; and any man who says to his brother, Thou fool, must answer for it in hell fire. If thou art bringing thy gift, then, before the altar, and rememberest there that thy brother has some ground of complaint against thee, leave thy gift lying there before the altar, and go home; be reconciled with thy brother first, and then come back to offer thy gift. If any man has a claim against thee, come to terms there and then, while thou art walking in the road with him; or else it may be that the claimant will hand thee over to the judge, and the judge to the officer, and so thou wilt be cast into prison. Believe me, thou shalt not be set at liberty until thou hast paid the last farthing.

You have heard that it was said, Thou shalt not commit

adultery. But I tell you that he who casts his eyes on a woman so as to lust after her has already committed adultery with her in his heart. (MATTHEW v: 20-28)

That fifth chapter of St. Matthew—how obvious it all is, how we take it all for granted. And yet, if you sit down and read it, it makes your hair stand on end. Oh, it's all perfectly simple and straightforward; it's part of the agreed syllabus—in fact, it more or less *is* the agreed syllabus; it's what the ordinary man means by Christianity. And yet on the face of it what it says is that if you behave as about ninety-nine per cent of the human race behaves, you shall in no case enter into the kingdom of heaven. Simple if you like, but isn't it rather exacting?

Our Lord has told us that his yoke is easy, his burden is light; how is it, then, that when he climbs up on to the mount of the beatitudes he promulgates a new law which surpasses, which boasts of surpassing, the law of Moses in its severity? Our justice, he says, our notion of what is due from man to God and from man to man, has got to give better measure than the justice of the scribes and Pharisees. All very well for them to avoid murdering people, we've got to go one better than that, we've got to avoid losing our tempers, if we want to get into the kingdom of heaven. Even our angry looks bring us before a summary court; if we utter an angry word, it has got to go to the assizes. I used to go to confession to a dear old priest who kept up a sort of running commentary all the time; and I remember when I said I'd been impatient sometimes when I was interrupted at my work he put in "Naturally." But our Lord doesn't say that; he says "anybody who is angry with his brother." Anybody who is angry with his brother is guilty, under the new law, of the same kind of offense which murder was under the old.

That is simple Christianity; that's what we've got to teach the delinquent boys in the Borstal schools. And of course it doesn't apply only to murder, it runs all through the commandments; the whole of the rest of the chapter is about that. Under the new law, just a look, at the street corner, is constructive adultery. The whole system has been tightened up; false swearing? That's nothing, you oughtn't to swear at all. Stealing? You mustn't even try to recover what is yours. And so on. That is the light burden, the easy yoke, we Christians have to bear.

Well, we naturally set to and try to get out of the difficulty. Perhaps, we suggest, our Lord was warning us against the danger of the first move, the first slip into temptation; after all, one thing does lead to another. That's why he tells us that the man who is angry with his brother is *in danger* of the judgement; he doesn't know what harm it may lead to in the long run. There was that priest who smacked an altar-boy over the head because he had made a fool of himself serving Mass, and the boy vowed he would never go to church again. Nothing very uncommon about that; only the boy was Marshal Tito, so it wasn't so good. And no doubt our Lord *was* concerned to put us on our guard against indulging our passions, because an uncontrolled temper (for example) may lead to such disastrous results. But that wasn't all. The word "danger," you see, is a misleading translation both of the Latin and of the Greek. Our

Lord means, there's no disputing it, that the man who is angry with his brother becomes then and there liable to the same penalties as did, under the old law, the murderer.

No, we've all got a better way out of it than that; you have to distinguish, we say, between precepts and counsels. "Thou shalt do no murder" is a precept, binding everybody everywhere under pain of mortal sin; if you break it, you lose God's friendship, and are no longer in a state of grace. Whereas a counsel is recommended to those who are striving after perfection, as a means towards attaining that end. When we are told not to resist evil, to turn the other cheek and let the robber take away our overcoat with the coat inside it, all that is a recommendation only, not a command. If we want to follow our Lord in the way of perfection, we shall have to behave like that, but not under any compulsion—we are not *bound* to do it. Chapter five of St. Matthew was only meant for the *élite* of Christians; not for the rough-and-tumble, not for you and me; the whole context shows that.

There is, to be sure, a certain doubt about what is meant by the rubric at the beginning of it. A great multitude had followed our Lord; so he went up on to the mountain-side; there he sat down, and his disciples came about him. And he began speaking to them—to whom? At first sight, we might think it was the multitudes, but you've only got to read on a little to see that that won't do. Our Lord says, only a few verses lower down, "You are the salt of the earth"; and again, "You are the light of the world." What, these inquisitive thousands who had come out to see the new prophet, hoping that with any luck he might cure them of their rheumatism—were they the salt of the earth? Were they the light of the world? Of course not; "he spoke to *them*" means that he spoke to the holy apostles, who were going to be his special friends, to live and die in close imitation of him. They were to turn the other cheek when the persecutor maltreated them; it was a special vocation they had. Try to make the fifth chapter of St. Matthew into a rule for all Christians, and you turn into an Anabaptist or a pacifist or a Communist at once.

We all know that that's true; but I wonder if it's the whole truth? After all, our Lord does say that we can't enter the kingdom of heaven unless our justice gives better measure than the justice of the scribes and Pharisees; and I think it's difficult to doubt that this utterance of his is meant to give the key to the whole chapter. He doesn't say we shall be rather second-rate citizens, that we shall take a very low place in the kingdom of heaven; he says we shan't get *in*. Was he, then, only legislating for his apostles, was he only talking to an *élite*? I don't personally think St. Matthew means that our Lord went up on to the mountain-side so as to leave the multitude behind; that he said, "Come away, I've got something special to say to you; it won't do for all these people." If you look at the end of chapter 7, where the sermon on the mount concludes, you will read "When Jesus had finished these sayings, the multitudes found themselves amazed at his teaching."

Oughtn't we perhaps to think of him as selecting the mountain-side precisely because, in some hollow of it, you could make your voice carry to a crowd of people? Oh, the apostles were in front; we know that; it says "his disciples came about him." No doubt he was talking to them; but are we certain that he was not talking *at* the multitude at the same time? Of course, they wouldn't make much of it, most of them; he was speaking in parables, as he always did. But they weren't told to put their fingers in their ears; "listen, you that have ears to hear with"—that was our Lord's principle. He meant, don't you think, that everybody who was within ear-shot, including the multitudes, should carry something away, even if it wasn't much.

I hope you see what I'm getting at. I can't help feeling that we've got it too much in water-tight compartments, this business about counsels and precepts; we Catholics have such a passion for water-tight compartments. I feel we're rather like those people at the big railway stations, sitting over a microphone and making a most hideous noise so that you can't hear yourself say your office. "Passengers for the slow train to Didcot will proceed from platform number six"—you know the kind of thing; and when I look at a moral theology book I get rather the same kind of impression about counsels and precepts, they're like the fast train and the slow train from Swindon to Didcot, and it's most important not to get into the wrong one. What a terrible lot of our time we priests spend in telling people what they *needn't* do; "Oh, no," we find ourselves saying, "you're not *bound* to do that," and one sometimes longs to add, "But you'll be a skunk if you don't." No, no (we say), it isn't a precept, it's only a counsel—I shouldn't read the sermon on the mount if I were you, it will only give you scruples. Don't we perhaps rather too much think of the counsels of perfection as something which need not be attempted—unless, of course, you are that kind of person? I never quite know whether it is the clergy or the laity that are responsible for it; but it is extraordinary what unheroic advice passes day by day through the grille of the confessional. Oh yes, I know we must be on our guard against presumption; we mustn't try to fly without wings— mustn't, in a more popular phrase, bite off more than we can chew. But is it really like that, this business of following the sermon on the mount? Is it really a question of the things we do, and not rather of the spirit in which we do them?

The spirit in which we do them—surely that is what this fifth chapter of St. Matthew is really about. We mustn't conceive the mount of the beatitudes as if it were a new Sinai, covered all over with notice-boards, only more of them. Sinai, I mean saying, "Thou shalt not kill, thou shalt not steal, thou shalt not covet," and then a whole fresh lot of boards put up saying, "Thou shalt not be angry," "Thou shalt not call people Raca," "Thou shalt not say Thou fool." Our Lord did say that his yoke was easy, that his burden was light, and he meant it. So that when he says, "Your justice must give fuller measure than the justice of the scribes and Pharisees" the point is not that we should feel bound to do a whole lot of things the scribes and Pharisees didn't. The point is that we should go about the business of living as God wants us to live in a spirit which the scribes and the Pharisees never dreamed of.

Am I giving a private interpretation of what our Lord said? That would be a dangerous thing to do. But I am not giving my own interpretation of it, I am giving St. Paul's interpretation about it. Such a lot of St. Paul's teaching is devoted to contrasting the spirit of Christ with the spirit of the Law, that and nothing else. "The spirit you have now received is not, as of old, a spirit of slavery, to govern you by fear; it is the spirit of adoption, which makes us cry out Abba, Father. . . . All the commandments are resumed in this one saying, Thou shalt love thy neighbour as thyself. . . . Learn to live and move in the spirit; then there is no danger of your giving way to the impulses of corrupt nature. . . . The Spirit yields a harvest of love, joy, peace and so on; no law can touch such lives as these. . . . Order your lives in charity, upon the model of that charity which Christ showed to us, when he gave himself up on our behalf"—you could go on for ever quoting St. Paul in this sense. I know that foolish sectaries have drawn dangerous conclusions from his doctrine, but it shines out clear for all that.

The Christian life is not a matter of consulting notice-boards; it means living by the law of love. And Christendom is not divided up into two water-tight compartments, the people who want to attain perfection and the people who don't want to do anything of the kind. Christendom consists of people who are trying to live by the law of love which Christ gave us, only some of us are doing it better than others. That is the point.

Read through that chapter of St. Matthew again, with St. Paul's epistles as your book-marker, and you will see that it isn't really meant to be a series of almost impossible prohibitions, inviting us to scruple. What was wrong with the scribes and Pharisees wasn't so much that they didn't

keep enough commandments as that they kept the commandments in a wrong spirit; in a niggling, haggling sort
of spirit, determined to see how much they could indulge
their own appetites and work off grudges against their
neighbour without actually infringing the letter of the law.
And that, our Lord tells us, is not the way to set about
getting into the kingdom of heaven. The kingdom of heaven
has its own court etiquette, and it is the law of love.

If and in so far as you are living by the spirit of the new
law, you will love your neighbour as yourself, you will see
his point of view with the same clearness as your own—
he will be a real person to you. And if his conduct inter-
feres in some way with your convenience, you won't need
to be told not to murder him. You won't even be angry;
or at least you won't burst out into some silly explosion of
anger; even if he is being a fool you won't tell him that he
is a fool, because obviously that won't do any good. You
won't need to consult a code of law; you will react Christ-
wise to the situation.

And it's the same all through the commandments. You
won't need to be cautioned about adultery or sins against
purity, because you will have too much reverence for the
rich, living thing marriage is, for the bright, delicate thing
purity is, to think even remotely of doing an injury to
either. You won't need to tie yourself down by oaths or
promises, because your love of truth will be too strong to
let you practise deceit on your neighbour, oath or no oath,
promise or no promise. You won't need to sit down and
calculate exactly whether your neighbour is infringing your
rights, whether to avenge yourself for an injury or a slight.

Your whole instinct, if and in so far as you live by the new law, will be to give and to forgive.

If only we could learn to picture ourselves as standing there on the mountain-side—at the back, of course, right at the back, where we belong, but still feeling that some of the sermon was meant for us! Or rather that it was all meant for us, but in our own measure. Our Blessed Lady and the saints are there in the front row, drinking it all in, finding it apparently quite easy—turn the other cheek? What else could you do? Take no thought for the morrow? Of course not, it would be ridiculous—and so on. Seeing them take it like that, we get discouraged; "oh, of course, they're *saints*," we say; and we are tempted to stop listening and get on with our sandwiches. But, you see, we've got it wrong; we *will* think about the impossibility of doing what the saints did, instead of wondering how they managed to do it.

Take even a person who's never been canonized, like Father Damien; when you hear about the way he lived among the lepers at Molokai you say to yourself, "Well, I hand it to him; *I* couldn't do a thing like that." And you feel discouraged, faintly jealous, almost annoyed, at being outclassed in this way. But you've got it all wrong; what is significant for you about the life of the heroic Christian is not what he did, but the spirit in which he did it. You can't imagine Damien going about saying to himself, "Dear me, how unpleasant this place is, and how very repulsive these people are! Of course, I know I have got to do it, because it is my duty; but I do wish my duty was to do something else!" He did it cheerfully; he liked doing it, because he loved Jesus Christ, and loved the image of the divine in those bodies which had almost lost the semblance of humanity. He walked by the way of love, by the spirit of the new law.

And that spirit is within our reach, even if the heroisms are not. We lose sight of the motive which animated the saints, because we are so dazzled by the scale of their achievement. That is why Saint Thérèse of Lisieux has exercised such a profound influence on our generation; she specialized in doing the ordinary things sublimely, and the ordinary things are all that most of us can do. The ordinary things—dull jobs, minor problems, contacts with unimportant people—can be done in a spirit of bondage, or in the spirit of love. "Listen," our Lord says, "you that have ears to hear with," and, more arrestingly, "Take this in, you whose hearts are large enough for it"; only the saints possess full receptivity, but the message is the same for all; for us, too, on the outskirts of the crowd, if we will listen. There is no need for us to be always dragging a log, to find living the Christian life an ungrateful business. Love is the talisman.

And when we say "love," don't let us think of the emotional transports which the saints have felt, which others besides the saints have felt, ecstasies of happiness, paroxysms of tears. All that is a side issue; the love of God belongs not to the emotions but to the will. Some of the greatest saints have persevered in loving God when they found no encouragement, no lightness of heart about doing it; St. Francis of Sales did it for years, in spite of a firm conviction that he was lost. It lies with your will, under the assistance of God's ordinary graces, to meet all the claims which life makes on you in the spirit of a lover. "No, I will not drive a hard bargain with God; always asking for soft options, always eager to do the least he demands of me, always reminding myself that it is not quite time I went into church yet, that So-and-so, who is bothering me for a favour, has no real claim on me. I want to give God more than the little he asks; more, if that were possible, than his due. "My God, set me free from the bondage of unwilling service and calculating piety; bring me out, here and now, into the glorious liberty of your sons."

12 Kindness

How many people in the New Testament, apart from our Blessed Lord, are described as "good men"? Only two; and a rather unexpected couple—St. Joseph of Arimathea, and St. Barnabas. In both cases St. Luke is the historian. And I think you get the impression in each case that here was a man of great good nature who came forward and did the thing that had got to be done, when it looked as if nobody else was prepared to do it.

St. Joseph comes quite suddenly on the scene; he is not mentioned anywhere else in the New Testament; he has never made any particular claim on the devotion of Christendom, has no feast in the calendar of the universal Church. And yet what he did, if you come to think of it, took some doing. To beard the Roman governor, to face unpopularity with the other Jewish rulers, to carry out the entombment rather promptly, between three and six o'clock on Good Friday afternoon, using his own grave for the purpose; it's odd that he should have commanded so little attention. But St. Luke, anyhow, has written his epitaph in brief; "he was a good man"—reacted to the needs of the moment, and didn't make any unnecessary fuss about it.

So with St. Barnabas; he was an apostle, but his feast doesn't take rank with the feasts of the other apostles, and it has nearly always been knocked out hitherto by one octave or another; he has very few churches dedicated to him. But he was the man who really discovered St. Paul; what a discovery! When the other apostles left St. Paul severely alone, a new convert who might, for all they knew, be a spy, an *agent provocateur*, it was St. Barnabus who brought him forward and insisted that the Church should take some notice of him. "He was a good man," St. Luke says again; he saw that this shy, rather difficult convert had got to be brought out a little and put on the map. Our Lord said it was hard for a rich man to enter the kingdom of heaven; but St. Joseph and St. Barnabus were both rich men, and both good men all the same.

How they haunt the mind with a sense of refreshment, those sudden phrases thrown out, as if at random, by the sacred authors! Like a breath of sea air—*Christi bonus odor*. I wanted to say something to you about what seems at first sight, and perhaps is, a very hackneyed subject; the pleasure which we can give to the Sacred Heart of our Lord by going out of our way to do acts of kindness to our fellow-men.

We feel we have heard too much of the subject, so that we are tired of it; it reminds us of Edwardian poetesses like Wilhelmina Stitch and Ella Wheeler Wilcox, all that business about helping lame dogs over stiles, "Smile a little, smile a little, as you go along," and all the rest of it. It has so often been proposed to us as a substitute for religion that we have almost begun to doubt whether it has anything to do with religion. There are so many people we know who would hardly call themselves Christians, and yet are undeniably good-natured people—"good-natured," doesn't the very word suggest that there is something unsupernatural about it? Human kindness is apt to seem more gracious, and to be more welcome, when it springs from a kind of instinct in us, than when it is the result of laborious speculation about whether it isn't our duty, as Christians, to do this or that. . . . And then there are the Boy Scouts, turning the whole thing into a joke with this talk about good deeds.

Well, if we argue like that, we are quite obviously in the wrong. Just because we haven't got a monopoly of Christian behaviour, we mustn't think it doesn't matter whether we behave as Christians or not. Just because other people, differently constituted from ourselves, seem to make the world a more cheerful place without thinking about it, that's no reason why you and I should leave the world as gloomy a place as ever, for want of thinking about it. Anyhow, we're going to think about it now.

Our Lord himself has summed the position up for us in a famous phrase. "Do to other men all that you would have them do to you; that is the law and the prophets." What would you say if somebody asked you to make that phrase clearer, by giving a concrete example? Probably you would say something like this: "Well, I don't like having rubbish shot in my front garden by the passers-by; so I don't throw my empty cigarette-packet into somebody else's garden. It makes me angry when people try to gatecrash the bus-queue, so I don't try and sneak in myself when I think nobody's looking. I don't like to have my character pulled to pieces behind my back, so I try not to pull other people's characters to pieces behind their backs. That's the sort of thing our Lord means, isn't it, when he tells us to do as we would be done by?"

Yes, all that's very illuminating. I don't mean that it illuminates the sermon on the mount; I mean that it illuminates your own outlook. You have given an admirable exposition of what our Lord would have meant if he had said, "Don't do to other men any of the things you wouldn't have them do to you." But he didn't say that; he said "*Do* to other men all that you *would* have them do to you." He said something positive, and you've turned it into something negative. You were thinking of Saturday night, and the list you would have to make up of the bad things you had done. As usual, you weren't thinking about the good things you might do. But our Lord wasn't like that; his teaching was positive, affirmative. "In him," as St. Paul tells us, "all is affirmed with certainty."

And one of the most important things about the sermon on the mount, if not the most important thing about the sermon on the mount, is just that, as I was trying to show you. It's all too easy to read the law and the prophets as if they were simply a long list of the things you mustn't do; but how inadequate that is! The law and the prophets tell you that you mustn't defraud a labourer of his wages. But I tell you to do to other people the sort of things that would make you feel happy if they were done to you. Imagine yourself a labourer, going home to his wife; what would be the best bit of news you could pass on to her? Why, if he could tell her "The boss gave me a bonus today." Very well, give him a bonus; you can afford to make a fellow-creature happy. That is what the law and the prophets were really getting at.

So let us get one thing clear from the start; we are not talking about sins; we are not discussing what sins of omission are worth mentioning in the confessional. We're trying to see whether we can't, for the love of our Lord, imitate his saints in going out of our way to be nice to people; imitate St. Joseph of Arimathea, by rising promptly to the occasion and doing the thing that needs doing when it hasn't occurred to anybody else; imitate St. Barnabas by meeting the awkward situation tactfully, and making much of the man who is left out in the cold. Things of that kind; supposing, I mean, that an angel came to you and said, "For the next fortnight you are not to confess your sins when you go to bed; you are to recount the good deeds you have performed during the day," it would be a bit of a facer, wouldn't it, however many badges you got in your scouting days?

Most of us find, I think, that those good deeds are rather like the fish your angling friends tell you about, the fish that got away. Or like what the French call the *esprit de l'escalier*, the brilliant retort that occurs to you just when you've said good-night, and are at the bottom of the staircase. That old woman at the side of the road—she was obviously going your way, and you had half a mind to offer her a lift, only somehow you didn't, and here you are, a couple of miles on. That word of encouragement you nearly uttered, but just didn't utter, to the friend who was going off to hospital. That change they gave you in the shop, which seemed at the time rather too much—was it too much? Anyhow, it's too late to go back now. How they haunt us, these frustrated acts of benevolence! What is it in us, that prevents us doing the right thing at the right moment?

In our humility, we shall be inclined to say, "Just idleness." But I don't think, with most of us, it *is* exactly idleness that paralyses our moral initiative. Impossible to deny that a great deal of the good we don't do is lost through idleness, when we refuse some invitation or neglect some opening that might have made all the difference. But this we do, commonly, at leisure, and with our eyes open; we discuss the pro's and con's of the case, and our summing-up is "I'm hanged if I can be bothered." But what I'm thinking of at the moment is the opportunities which take us by surprise, don't give us time to examine our motives like that. And I think there are three reasons, in the main, for which we are apt to lose these opportunities. One is want of imagination. One is want of alacrity. And one is want of courage.

Want of imagination—you can see at once what a lot that has to do with it, because our Lord himself calls upon us for an exercise of the imagination; "Do to all men all that you would have them do to you"—how *would* you want to be treated, if you were in their case? Of course, it's not difficult to see that a man who has fallen into a canal wants to be pulled out, or that a small boy crying in the street is upset about something; no imagination needed there. But—take my favourite test case of considerateness; have you ever reflected how unpleasant it must be to be permanently crippled, so that you can only just hobble along when other people can bustle about as they like? If you have, I think your instinct will be to reduce speed when you overtake a cripple in the street, unless you are in a legitimate hurry; you will want to pass him at about two miles an hour, so as not to remind him too forcibly of the advantages you enjoy. That is a tiny instance, and perhaps you will think it a foolish one. But it's a good test, I think, of considerateness.

Deaf people, how they get left out in conversation! Don't neglect the deaf, even if it does make you feel a fool shouting at them. An old woman, sitting by herself in a corner; do you realize how old people like to be taken notice of? Anybody can be kind to children, and get good marks by it, but they can be perfectly happy, really, playing their own games on the floor; it is grandmamma, left in the window-seat with her knitting and her memories, conscious that people think her rather a bore, who will be really grateful, even for a word or two.

Remember how our Lord commended the dishonest steward, because he was wiser in his generation than Christians are, when they don't make friends of the poor against the day of judgement. It isn't only the poor, with their financial needs, who have that kind of claim on us. It's all the people who feel odd man out; the invalid who likes to be asked about his health, the shy, plain girl whom nobody pays any attention to, the unsuccessful author who longs to meet somebody who has heard of his book, and so on—if you put yourself in their place, you will realize that they ought to come on your list of charity as Priority No. 1.

And remember, when our Lord tells us to do as we would be done by, he doesn't mean us to imagine that everybody is made exactly like ourselves, and will enjoy exactly what we ourselves enjoy. Your idea of a large evening may be to go out for a spin in the car; it doesn't follow that you perform an act of charity by forcing that form of recreation on a guest who hates it, but is too shy to refuse. Kindness can easily be misplaced; middle-aged men don't, as a rule, like to be called "Sir," or to be helped on with their overcoats; it makes them feel old. There is an art, too, in not overdoing one's hospitality; not embarrassing people by still pressing another helping on them when they've already refused twice. If we know people really well, and are really fond of them, how instinctively we allow for their feelings! If we are looking out for a job, and wanting to make a good impression, how carefully we study the tastes of the man whose good word is important to us! To go about the world allowing for the feelings of comparative strangers, studying the tastes of people whose good word will be no sort of use to you on this side of the grave—that is to treat others as we would like them to treat us.

And then the next thing is the want of alacrity. It is extraordinary, isn't it, how much quicker off the mark some people are than others? I suppose build and temperament have a great deal to do with it; but I think if we find we are of the slow-moving sort we can do something, and are all the better for it if we do something, to change our habits. To be mobile, to be always on the alert—that's a thing that can do no harm to any of us. Our Lord tells us to have our loins girt; he is talking, I suppose, chiefly about our eternal destinies when he says that; but I think he likes to see us ready and watching even for the smallest opportunity of serving him in his members.

The habit we don't want to get into is the habit of the arm-chair. I don't mean that we ought never to sit in an arm-chair; but there are some people who get so wrapped up in the thing they are doing, even if it's just reading the newspaper or sewing on a button, that when you address a remark to them and they say "Oh, yes" you know they haven't really heard; or rather your remark hasn't really registered. Of course if you are adding up figures, or playing bridge, you must give a certain amount of concentration to it; but there are people who get so wrapped up in quite unexacting occupations that they don't seem to be able to stop. And people who are like that will always find that opportunity has passed them by; the kind word was on the tip of their tongues, but it never managed to get across; the suggestion which would have saved so much trouble was made, but it was only shouted out of the window when the other person was out of ear-shot.

"He has eyes upon all his company"—that is how Cardinal Newman begins his definition of a gentleman; and I think there's something to be said for that, you know. It's all very well to be absent-minded, but not to the point of forgetting that there are other people in the room. Be on the alert to do service to others, and stay on the alert till you are quite sure you have finished. Somebody has asked you the way, and you've told him, but he looks the helpless sort of person who would get it wrong. Just watch him down the road, and see, anyhow, that he starts right.

And finally the want of courage. How familiar we are

with that, some of us anyhow, in quite trivial and un-dignified connexions! The person opposite you in the bus has got his tie coming out at the side of his collar; and yet he looks as if he were dressed for an occasion; perhaps he is going to be interviewed for a job, and that's the sort of thing which may tell against him—have you the courage to produce that sentence which begins "Excuse me, Sir"? He can't really take offence; and it wouldn't matter if he did, but somehow it needs an enormous effort with one's vocal chords to get past the "Excuse me, Sir." That's only an *ad absurdum* illustration; quite often it does need a real effort of moral courage to do the right thing—or isn't it the right thing? There's so much to be said on both sides.

Sometimes it takes courage to risk interfering in other people's lives, even when there's plenty of time to think it over. So-and-so is contemplating a course of action which you think will be dangerous for him; should you warn him? Or will it do no good? So-and-so is hard up, and you would like to help him out; but can you, without his taking offence? Letter after letter is written, and torn up. But much worse, when you have to make your decision all in a moment—tell a person, for example, a comparative stranger, that he must stop drinking, or he won't be fit to drive his car. It's not your business, exactly, and he will probably tell you so in no uncertain terms. But somebody's got to do it; and you may be the person God means to do it. Not a sin to keep silence, but . . . well, here is your chance.

I don't want to make you scrupulous about all this. Still less do I want to turn you into the kind of person who is always interfering here, there and everywhere, finding things which people haven't lost and offering helpful suggestions to people who can get on perfectly well without them. But it *is* a curious fact, if you come to think of it, that our Lord only once gave us anything like a full-dress picture of the Last Judgement, at the end of the twenty-fifth chapter of St. Matthew; and in that picture the souls of men are not judged quite as you would expect. No reference is made to the evil they did or didn't do; only to the good they didn't do or did. "He went about doing good"—that is St. Peter's epitaph on his Divine Master; perhaps we should translate, "he went through the world doing good," with the implication that that wasn't precisely what he came into the world *for*, but he did it all the same, just in passing. He came to bring us the adoption of sons, and to save us by his death; but wherever he went, he would heal the sick and cast out devils—couldn't help it, you might almost say; the theologians tell us, don't they, that good is *diffusivum sui*, it has a natural tendency to spread itself.

And although the primary business of every Christian is to save his soul by identifying his will with the will of God for him, he has to pass through a world of human beings in doing so, and even when it is not precisely his job, even where he is not responsible for the people with whom he comes in contact, if he is a true disciple of his Master, he goes about doing good; the eyes of his fellow-men light up at his coming, and their tears embalm his memory.

I3 Humility

I want to talk about humility, and especially as it affects us in our human relations. I mean, when people have treated us badly, or when we think they have, we feel aggrieved and indignant about it, telling ourselves that we, of all people in the world, ought not to have been treated in this particular way by this particular person. By the time we have brooded over it for twenty minutes, injury has taken on the colour of insult, and pride has got control. To be sure, you may call it a fault of charity in us, rather than a fault of humility; but just here, charity and humility are very close neighbours; and I think we have a better chance of restoring ourselves to a good temper by telling ourselves not to be absurd, than by trying to see—let alone to take—the other person's point of view.

It is that kind of humility that St. Paul recommends to the church at Philippi. They had raised a subscription and sent it to St. Paul, who was then a prisoner at Rome; so his letter to the Philippians is a thank-letter, but he has one or two other things to say to them as well. "I call upon thee, Evodia, and I call upon thee, Syntyche, to make common cause in the Lord"—evidently they weren't. It's one of the most comforting things about the New Testament, the more you read it the more conscious you are that the early Christians quarrelled among themselves almost as much as we do. We have no idea who Evodia and Syntyche were; some commentators think Evodia was a man, Evodias, and Syntyche was his wife; but I don't think there's anything to support that theory except that, as I say, they didn't get on. No, I think they were just two ladies engaged in good works; probably one of them wanted to send the offering to St. Paul in money, and the other wanted to send it in kind, and after that they didn't speak.

It was for the benefit of these people and of people like them that he began his second chapter with that great exhortation to humility which we all know so well. He tells them they ought to think with the same mind, cherish the same bond of charity; "You must never act in a spirit of factiousness, or of ambition; each of you must have the humility to think others better men than himself." And then, with a sudden swoop into theology, of which only St. Paul would be capable, he goes on, "Yours is to be the same mind which Christ Jesus showed. His nature is, from the first, divine, and yet he did not see, in the rank of Godhead, a prize to be coveted; he dispossessed himself, and took the nature of a slave, fashioned in the likeness of men" and so on. That great hymn of the Incarnation, which theologians have been quoting and probing ever since—we owe it, humanly speaking, to the circumstances that one or two pious ladies at Philippi weren't pulling together. How like St. Paul! Impossible to say, again and again, what turned his thoughts in a particular direction!

At least, is it quite impossible here? We've always got to

remember that St. Paul wrote his letters to real places, to real people. And we are in a position to know, from the Acts of the Apostles, what happened when he first went to Philippi. He got into trouble with some slave-owners, who dragged him before the magistrates, and the magistrates beat him and put him in prison without trial, neither of which things they had any right to do, because he was a Roman citizen. He didn't mention that at the time; he only mentioned it the next day, when they sent the order for his release. I wonder if he didn't perhaps remember all that, when he sat down to write his letter to the people at Philippi, and told them not to be always standing on their dignity, always claiming their rights? It may be, when the sentence of scourging was pronounced, it occurred to St. Paul that he had only got to say three words, CIVIS ROMANUS SUM, and the whole proceedings would have to be stopped. And perhaps he thought to himself, "Well, of course I am a Roman citizen; but is the citizenship of an empire like this really anything to write home about? Wouldn't it really be more worthy of a Christian to carry on as if I were the slave they take me for? After all, the Christ I serve was God, and yet he didn't see, in the rank of Godhead, a prize to be coveted; he dispossessed himself, and took the nature of a slave; there is an example to follow!" All *that* St. Paul remembers, in his Roman prison, and he pours out on to the paper in front of him, for the benefit of the Philippians, the same thoughts which had occurred to him, long before, at Philippi.

You or I, if we wanted to set before our minds some example of humility that was centred in the person of our

Blessed Lord, would probably think of him as working in the carpenter's shop, under St. Joseph's orders, or as accepting baptism from St. John in the Jordan, or as carrying his cross on the Via Dolorosa. But St. Paul will go to the heart of things; he will take his model of humility not from the Incarnate, but from the Incarnation. That God should express himself in human terms at all—that was the supreme condescension; in St. Paul's thought, our Lord seems to walk straight from Bethlehem to Calvary, taking all those other humiliations in his stride. At one stroke, God dispossessed himself, laid aside, as it were, the trappings of royalty and came to live among his slaves as a slave; after that, what further humiliation could there be except that final act of obedience by which he, the immortal, died?

How splendidly the Credo at Mass brings that out! All those rolling phrases which describe to us what the Divine Word is, "the only-begotten Son of God, by the Father engendered before time began; God sprung from God, Light sprung from Light, true God as from true God he came," and so on. And then, *qui propter nos homines*, "who for love of us men"! God is the last end of man; as the coat exists for the sake of him who wears it, as the tool exists for the sake of him who uses it, so man exists for the sake of God; there is no other justification for his being there at all. And when God becomes Man at the Incarnation, the mystery isn't merely how that happened, how two Natures could be united in a single Divine Person. The mystery is also why it happened; man exists for the sake of God, but when God became Man he did it for the sake of man. *Propter nos homines;* what marvel that when those words reach us, we get ready to fall on our knees?

But these immensities strike the ear rather than the mind; they are too deep, most of us find, for meditation. Our Lord knew that, and I expect that is why, at the very close of his life, he made a most gracious gesture by which he dramatized the doctrine of the Incarnation in a form we could all of us understand. I mean, when he washed his disciples' feet at the Last Supper. It's one of those curious instances where you can only get at the full story by reading two different gospels; they dovetail into one another, each supplies the gap the other left. At the Last Supper, St. Luke tells us, the disciples were discussing which of them should be the greatest. What extraordinary disciples our Lord had! I suppose it must have arisen out of the arrangement of the table at supper. Anyhow, we all know the words in which he silenced their dispute, "Tell me, which is greater, the man who sits at table, or the man who serves him? Surely the man who sits at table; yet I am among you as your servant." And then—surely it must have been then—he rose from his place—St. John is our authority for this—girded himself with a towel, and began to wash their feet. *Propter nos homines;* he took the nature of a slave. And then, for fear they might not have understood what he said a few minutes earlier, he draws the moral, "Why then, if I have washed your feet, I who am the Master and the Lord, you in your turn ought to wash one another's feet."

As usual, the kingdom of heaven has turned everything upside down; the old struggle for precedence is to go on, but in a new form; he who would be the greatest of all must be the servant of all. Because we worship a God who dispossessed himself, every Christian must dispossess himself, become the slave of the rest. Oh, it sounds dreadfully simple, all this, dreadfully obvious. But tell me, when did you last do it?

It isn't a simple thing, the virtue of humility. It is one of the natural virtues, and yet you might almost say that it was completely hidden until revelation revealed it to us; the heathens didn't give it a place in the list of the virtues at all, and if you look up *humilitas* in the Latin dictionary you will find the meanings given are "lowness, meanness, insignificance, littleness of mind, baseness, abjectness." After all, in the sheer logic of the thing, why should there be such a virtue at all? If you haven't got such and such a quality, you'd be a fool to pretend you have; better own up to your insufficiency. If you *have* got such and such a quality, where's the sense in pretending you haven't?

It savours rather of affectation when some great authority on wild flowers tells you that he used to botanize a bit at one time. After all, either you are a scratch player or you aren't. If you aren't, you're a fool to pretend that you are; you will only get found out. If you are, you cannot but admit the fact to yourself, and to others if you are questioned. Nobody wants you to be always reminding your friends of it, always lugging it into the conversation. But why bother about humility, as long as we keep a certain amount of modesty in our bearing? Why not tell the truth and shame the devil?

Well, of course we all know that that won't do as an account of the matter, even if you are only thinking about humility in conversation—which is only a small department of the subject. It is perfectly possible to realize your insufficiency, and to boast about it all the same. If you are very bad at golf you can proclaim the fact in a way which suggests to your audience, in the first place, that golf isn't much of a thing to be good at, and in the second place that you are such a busy person, hold such an important place in the community, that you can't afford to waste time on a mere game.

Have you ever noticed a curious thing about our modern tricks of language? Fifteen or twenty years back, if somebody asked you what was the longest bridge in the world, or some interesting question of that kind, you replied, "I don't know." Now, if you are faced with the same question, you reply, "I wouldn't know." It is a perfectly harmless affectation of speech; but the insinuation of it is surely just what we have been talking about. "I wouldn't know; that is not the sort of question to which you should expect an answer from a person like me. My researches into the distinction between essence and existence, or into the poetry of the later Middle Ages, do not leave me much time to go about measuring bridges. No doubt there are people who find calculations of that kind very absorbing; and I bear you no ill-will for pestering me on the subject, although the effect has been to expose my ignorance. I am, in a general way, a rather cultured sort of person, and if bridge-building statistics were part of the furniture of an enlightened mind, I should have been at pains to inform myself about the point you mention. But personally, I find them rather boring. I wouldn't know."

However, as I said at the beginning of this rather rambling discourse, I want to talk about a special kind of humility; the humility which gives us a right attitude towards our fellow-men by making us always want to take the lowest place among them. And here, too, the subject has its difficulties. When that extraordinary man, John Wesley, had been reading a passage of Bishop Jeremy Taylor, to the effect that a Christian ought to regard himself as the worst man in any company he visited, he disagreed, John Wesley did, and said that such "comparative humility" was "unreasonable." Now, here are two holy Protestants at issue; which was right?

Let us put it in a rather brutal form. You have been hoping to get some recognition, to be entrusted with some job, which seemed just right for you; and somebody else has got it instead. Now, you've obviously got to make the best of it; even the conventions of civilized society demand that you shouldn't go about running down the successful candidate; that will get you nowhere, even in this world. It is expected of you that you should say something about the best man winning. But what ought the interior attitude of the Christian to be, when he says that? Ought you to be so humble that you quite honestly believe the other candidate was the better candidate; if necessary, in defiance of the obvious facts? Or ought you to make an act of faith that he must have been the better candidate, in spite of appearances? Or are you allowed to retain your belief that you were the better candidate, but thank God that other people didn't realize it, and so have inflicted on you a welcome humiliation?

This last-named attitude sounds, to be sure, terribly priggish; I've put it in its most priggish form on purpose. But it is true, you see, that humility doesn't always call upon you to revise your opinions; it may call upon you simply to pocket them. After all, the model of humility which St. Paul put before the Philippians was our Lord himself; and our Lord himself, even as Man, couldn't think of himself as inferior to his fellow-men, couldn't join in the outcry which demanded Barabbas. But he did submit, willingly, to that monstrous act of injustice which preferred Barabbas to himself.

And it may be the business of a Christian to follow this example of divine humility, to let himself be put in the wrong even when he knows he is in the right, when he cannot, without affectation, pretend to himself that the facts are otherwise. Blame may be imputed to him which belongs to another, and he may be obliged, in charity, to shoulder it. Much more probably he will find that the advice he has offered has been overridden, and he is obliged in loyalty to follow out what he believes to be a mistaken policy. To do that in all simplicity; to work to another man's plan, which is not yours, whole-heartedly, not indemnifying yourself by moody discontents and cynical despairs—that takes a man who is humble with the humility of Christ.

Let us make no mistake about it, there *is* a human humility which ought to make us distrust our own judgement far more than we do. How often we have to admit, afterwards, that our judgement on such and such an occasion was absolutely wrong! But it doesn't prevent us having an equally robust confidence in our own judgement on the next occasion. How easy we find it to account for other people's odd behaviour, oh, quite charitably, by reference to their education or their home background or whatever it may be, without ever noticing that *we* have any prejudices, or that any explanation is demanded of them! When we contemplate the odd kinks in other people's minds we ought to start wondering about our own; instead, we always feel like the reasonable man.

And a great many of our heart-burnings arise out of slights which weren't meant to be slights at all. "I do think he might at least have written," we say; always watch yourself when you find yourself saying the words "I do think"; it means that you have lost your temper, or are just going to lose it. But there were a hundred reasons, I don't say good reasons, but understandable reasons, why he didn't write, if you only knew. . . . No, when all is said and done, it is a great part of humility to realize that there is nothing whatever to be humble about. No, your advice wasn't taken; but are you really sure it was good advice? Or anyhow, would anybody have expected it to be good advice, coming from you?

That is what I call human humility; and the more you can exercise it, so that you don't need to fall back upon divine humility, the better. It's apt to make rather prigs of us, if we are not careful, to be always offering things up. And I think it is at least arguable that the sacrifices which we make for God are most acceptable to him when we are not conscious of making them. But a time may come when all these outworks of human humility will be broken through, and you will find yourself thrown back on an inner line of defence. The claims of charity or of obedience may engage you to serve God in surroundings, and among people, wholly unsympathetic to you; every opinion of yours will be slighted, all your well-meant efforts to be of service will be criticized, the whole burden of maintaining some show of Christian charity among Christian people will be thrown upon your shoulders, and you will half despise yourself for your own submissiveness in tolerating the situation.

Heroic endurance, you feel, would come easier; it is to be everlastingly at the mercy of these pinpricks that gets you down. Yet your duty will be clear; there will be no way of cutting the knot legitimately open to you. Whether you can emerge from that test with your character unsoured, and your sense of humour unspoilt, will depend, I think, on whether you have been at pains to understand the meaning of the Incarnation, and to make its lesson your own. *Qui propter nos homines*, God coming down to be the slave of his creatures, God kneeling down and washing their feet, so that they, in their turn, may learn to wash one another's feet—nothing less than that divine humility is our target.

14 Simplicity

SIMPLICITY isn't at all a simple idea when you come across it in a religious connexion. There are contexts in which you get the impression that it is a *bad* thing to be simple; at the very beginning of the book of Proverbs, for example, Wisdom is represented as expostulating with the folly of mankind; "What (says she) are you still gaping there, simpletons?"—the word used in the Hebrew looks very much as if it meant, literally, going about with your mouth open, like the slang word *gobe-mouche* in French. Sometimes, on the contrary, you get the impression that it is a good thing to be simple; as when our Lord tells his apostles, according to the Douay Version, to be "wise as serpents and simple as doves." And sometimes it looks as if being simple was just part of your nature, part of your condition in life, like being poor instead of rich, delicate instead of robust; a thing you have got to make the best of. As, for example, when the psalm says, "The Lord cares for simple hearts, and to me, when I lay humbled, he brought deliverance"—you get the impression that God looks after simple people because they are quite incapable of looking after themselves. How exactly are we to pin down this complicated idea of simplicity?

Simplicity is one of the divine attributes; it comes first on the list; and we might suppose that we ought to imitate the simplicity of Almighty God just as we try to imitate the holiness of Almighty God. But of course that won't do. We can't in the strict sense imitate his simplicity any more than his omnipotence. That divine simplicity is something we mention with awe; it is a perfection, a splendour;—whereas, we don't think of human simplicity quite like that, do we? Not that we use the word in a contemptuous sense, meaning half-witted, as the Italians do; but always it has a slightly patronizing air about it. The native races, children saying their prayers, country-folk, especially when they are not our own country-folk—we call them "simple," and it gives us a nice broad-minded feeling. We, who have taken up the white man's burden, are so complicated in our outlook, see so many sides to a question, are so tied down in our behaviour by a hundred conventions of civilization; how delightful it would be to get away from all that, and go back to believing in fairies! We use the word "simple" as a compliment, but a rather left-handed compliment.

Well, why did our Lord tell his disciples to be as simple as doves? Innocent, perhaps, is the true rendering; but the Greek word does literally mean "unmixed," and it is contrasted, you see, with the wisdom of the serpent; somehow, Christ's apostles have got to be sophisticated people and unsophisticated people at one and the same time. He explains what he means, I think, in the verses which follow. They are to keep their wits about them, and not put their trust in men, who will only betray them to the persecutor. But, once betrayed, when they stand before the persecutor, they have no need to keep their wits about them; *then* they must go at it bald-headed, and leave it to the Holy Spirit to see that the answers they make are the right answers. We have our Lord's own word for it that sophistication isn't everything.

At the same time, there isn't much about simplicity in the New Testament; only a handful of references. Curiously, I think the word really owes its place in our devotional vocabulary to the *Imitation of Christ*. There, you will find some thirty references under "simple" and "simplicity," nearly all of them complimentary. To be simple, in the *Imitation*, is not just to be so helpless that Almighty God feels bound to look after you; it is to have a quality which God wants to see in us, and very often doesn't see in those distinguished theologians against whom, somehow, Thomas à Kempis seems to have a bit of a grudge. Yes, the word became part of our devotional vocabulary, but the possibilities of it weren't really discovered till just the other day, within the life-time of some of us.

St. Thérèse of Lisieux, so recent a saint that she isn't even mentioned in the *Catholic Encyclopaedia*—she wasn't even stop-press news in 1910—was the person who really put simplicity on the map. I can prove it; in the collect at Mass for the third of October, her feast, we ask that we may follow the footsteps of the holy virgin Thérèse in humbleness and simpleness of heart; and to the best of my knowledge it is the only place in the liturgy where that particular virtue is mentioned. You can't quite say that she invented it; but it was like her holy impudence to force it on the Church, wasn't it? The whole idea of the Spiritual Childhood is that we shouldn't just be innocent, as children are, we should be simple with the simplicity of children. She took us right back to the gospels, and referred us to the picture of our Lord blessing the children and taking them in his arms.

"Let the children be; do not keep them back from me; the kingdom of heaven belongs to such as these." How old were the children? They are generally depicted in art as about four or five. But the word St. Luke uses in this passage would only apply to infants in arms. You see, *we* like to sentimentalize about children; we are delighted by their pretty ways (when they *are* pretty) and the quaint things they say. We can construct a beautiful picture of heaven with children like that playing about in it. But that wasn't, if you come to think of it, what our Lord was talking about. Infants were brought to him in their mothers' arms, and the disciples wanted to give him a rest, but he wouldn't stop blessing them; the kingdom of heaven belongs (he said) to people like these. Not "belongs to these"; he wasn't concerned to tell us that heaven will be ninety per cent populated by infants, even if that were true. He was telling us that the grown-up people who go to heaven will be those who were *like* children. And of course he has put it more plainly elsewhere, "unless you become like little children again, you shall not enter the kingdom of heaven." We are to imitate, we grown-up people, the innocence of children; and (as St. Thérèse rightly saw) we are to imitate them also in their simplicity.

And that, you know, is rather a hard saying. Because our Lord is talking about people who *become* simple; not about people who *are* simple and go on being simple because they can't help it. Does God love children just because they are children? Does he love uneducated people just because they are uneducated? My own impression is that our Lord, and many of his saints after him, really loved the society of children because it reminded them of what grown-up people would be like if only they were innocent, if only they were simple. However, we mustn't stop to argue that. All I'm concerned to point out is that the moral of what our Lord said, in these two famous passages, was meant for people who weren't particularly innocent and weren't particularly simple, but had got to become so.

And that seems to me a hard saying because, whatever you think about innocence, to make yourself simple is obviously going to be a rather difficult process. Indeed, can you do it at all without being artificial? And is not artificiality the very opposite of simplicity? That extraordinary woman, Madame Guyon, was prepared to dress up in baby-clothes and talk baby-language in honour of the Sacred Infancy; is that really the kind of thing we are aiming at? Obviously that is absurd; it would be absurd if we all gave up our daily paper and took to reading comics instead.

And it isn't merely that we don't want grown-up people to behave childishly; we don't want educated people to behave as if they were less educated than they are. If they did, would they be a step nearer the kingdom of heaven? No, simplicity is something we find in children, find in plain country-folk; but it isn't the same thing as being childish, it isn't the same thing as being unexpensively educated. What is it, then? What is the quality which shines more brightly, perhaps, in the nursery and in the cottage, but doesn't take its character from either of them?

I think we ought to go back to a subject we dismissed rather hastily a few minutes ago, and say a little about the simplicity of God. Because it is a fixed rule of thought that you must always interpret the lower by the higher, not the higher by the lower. Not that we can ever begin to understand the nature of God; but the mere fact of contrasting the negative things we know about him with the positive things we know all too well about ourselves is often a wonderful discipline for the mind. God is absolutely simple —take that statement at its lowest. Concentrate your attention upon one single department of the perfection it implies, upon the fact that God is pure Spirit, instead of being compounded of body and soul, as we are—that, after all, is equally true of the holy angels. Even so, think of it! Think how continually we are hampered, you and I, between our getting up in the morning and our going to bed at night, by the mere fact that we are body and soul. That surge of discomfort, somewhere in the region of the chest, which ought to accompany, and to be dictated by, the God-given sense of indignation—how it gets out of control, and dominates us, when the Hoover next door interrupts us while we are at work, or when a candid friend passes on to us some criticism that has been made about us by somebody. And all that, because this apparatus for anger in us has got out of control, is directing our rational faculties instead of being directed by our rational faculties. . . . But there's no need to multiply instances; we all know how this composite-ness of ours, body-and-soul creatures, lets us down and shames us all the time. If only we were simple, if only we were like God, or even like the holy angels! But we aren't.

Always, when we have tried to understand our miserable human nature better by contrasting it with the divine, and got ourselves fogged in the process, we fall back on the contemplation of our Blessed Lord, perfect God and perfect Man. Was Jesus Christ simple? We can't take it for granted that he had *all* the perfections of our human nature, taken as they stand; he had, for example, no faith—he did not believe because he *saw*. Had he simplicity? Yes, although it sounds a ridiculous suggestion, if we think of simplicity as if it meant being undeveloped, being under-educated, the sort of thing we were saying just now. Our Lord Jesus Christ was perfectly simple, because he was perfectly integrated.

Do you remember where it says that the people of some Samaritan village would not entertain him, because his face was set as if he was going to Jerusalem? That phrase is a symbol of his whole career; his face was *set*, wasn't always turning this way and that, looking to see what other people were thinking about him, looking to see where his own advantage lay, looking to see what was the best opportunity for striking an impressive attitude, for coining a memorable phrase. No, his face was set towards Jerusalem; the cross was the baton in his knapsack.

Have we still pitched our meditation too high? Do we still find it difficult to get inside Jesus of Nazareth? Let us fall back on his saints, wholly human like ourselves; let us fall back on St. Thérèse, since it is she who has patented for us this idea of simplicity. She was simple, God knows she was simple; and on a hasty analysis we are tempted to say

that it was because she was just like a child—tell me, have
you ever known a child like St. Thérèse? No, her simplicity
lay in the fact that she was, as near as ordinary human nature
can go, integrated; she knew what she was out for, and was
determined to get it; every moment of every day was built
up, conscientiously, laboriously if you will, into a pattern;
every action of hers was a stitch in her divine needle-work,
her sampler, copied from the life of Jesus Christ. Her life,
so short, was so business-like; she cut out all the frills. And
the reason why it makes you and me so ashamed of ourselves
isn't really that she was young and natural and impulsive,
isn't really that she was French and had the French knack of
intimacy with the supernatural, but that she knew what she
was about, subordinated her whole life to a plan. She was
simple, because to her there was only one thing that
mattered; she wasn't being distracted from her aim all the
time by trifles and scruples, as we are.

Well, we have got, somehow, to go back and be like little
children; be simple with an effort, as little children are
effortlessly. How are we to set about it? I can only suggest
one or two ways in which we can—no, I won't say in which
we can improve our present form, because that perhaps
would be expecting too much. But one or two directions in
which we might keep a watch over ourselves, so as not to
become more complicated than we can help. Simplicity
means, when you get down to it, living for an end, and not
allowing yourself to be distracted by side-issues.

Here are three points only, among a multitude which we
could name; three suggestions about what you want to avoid,
if you aspire to follow Christ and his saints in their simplic-

ity. First of all—he was always going on at us about that—
worldly riches. Which means, I think, for most of us not
pounds, shillings and pence, but undue attachment to a
particular set of external objects and a particular way of
living. What makes us complicated when we would like to
be simple is not so much our possessions as our possessiveness.
I was reading only the other day how Benedict Joseph
Labre, that curious saint who preferred to live and die as a
down-and-out, gave up sleeping in the Coliseum and took to
spending the night in other corners of Rome because he
didn't want to get too much attached to one particular *form*
of lodging in the open air. Have you a special chair which
is *yours*, so that it makes you feel uncomfortable when a
visitor occupies it instead? Even a tiny thing like that can
be the enemy of simplicity. Don't multiply, as far as you
can help it, the number of things you can't do without.

And second—be yourself, don't pose, even in fun. Pull
yourself up, when you find that you are trying to make an
impression, trying to make yourself interesting, by proclaim-
ing an admiration for this, an aversion from that, which you
haven't really got. Don't be in a hurry to say the thing you
were going to say, without having considered it; let the other
person get his remark in first—it won't do any harm. Un-
reality of this sort isn't sinful, no, but it can grow upon you
and turn you into an artificial kind of person, not yourself.
Don't be one person to your fellow-men and another person
in your prayers.

And thirdly, learn to mind your own business. For the
welfare of certain human souls God will hold you, in your
degree, responsible; your family, your close friends, your

pupils if you are a teacher, your staff if you are an employer. They are your business. But each of us has a great penumbra of neighbours and casual acquaintances which falls outside this category altogether; you don't know such people well enough to have any influence on their lives, and yet their lives form an inexhaustible subject of gossip. You are continually wondering why So-and-so behaves as he or she does; whether such and such a marriage is a happy one; what is the real truth about a mysterious happening which doesn't concern you. All that sort of gossip encourages you to live in a mental world of unnecessary distractions and grievances which disturbs, however slightly, your peace of mind. And without peace of mind you can't be integrated; your own life is impoverished when your whole attention is squandered on the lives of other people.

But to be *really* simple—how wondeful that would be!

15 Faith and Results

I WANT to talk to you about that very difficult chapter, one
of the most difficult in the gospels, the sixth chapter of St.
John. We don't notice the difficulties of it, because we think
it's just an account of the miracle of the Five Thousand,
followed, naturally enough, by a discourse on the Blessed
Sacrament. All those phrases we know so well about eating
our Lord's flesh and drinking his blood, if we are to have
eternal life abiding in us—they all come from this chapter.
But St. John's Gospel is so curiously arranged that we can't
ever be quite certain on what occasion such and such a thing
was said; and there are scholars who believe—I think there
is a good deal to be said for their belief—that these familiar
phrases were used at some quite different time, very probably at the Last Supper, when they would clearly be in
place. Anyhow, that is not what this chapter is *about*. It
describes the miracle of the Five Thousand, who are so much
impressed by the miracle that they want to make our Lord
a king. He defeats their attempt by giving them the slip;
they think he has got no boat to get across the Lake in—
and of course he hasn't, but he walks on the water. Then,
next day, in the synagogue at Capharnaum, he shows them
where they were wrong.

If you read through the chapter, omitting a few verses which form the gospel for Corpus Christi Day (verses 56-59), and the three or four verses which precede them, you will find that the whole of it reads, not as a sacramental discourse, but as a discourse on the contrast between this life and eternity, with sacramental overtones coming in. And you will find that it exactly balances the conversation between our Lord and the woman of Samaria, in the fourth chapter of the same gospel. Just as he told the woman of Samaria that she ought to be asking him for living water, so here he tells the Jews that they are wrong if they only work to earn food which perishes in the using; what they really need is the living bread which comes down from heaven. The living water was not what Jacob dug up from his well; the living bread is not the manna which Moses found scattered about in the wilderness. Drink from Jacob's well, and you will soon be thirsty again; eat of the manna Moses gave, and it will only keep you going for a little; then you will die as your fathers died in the desert. He who drinks the living water will never thirst again; he who eats the living bread will live for ever. You see how the two conversations run on the same pattern all through; there are overtones of baptism in the one, Eucharistic overtones in the other; but they are only overtones. What our Lord is *saying* is that religion doesn't mean patriarchs digging wells, or law-givers grubbing up manna. It means piercing through the veils of sense, and making ourselves familiar, through faith, with the realities of a world of which we have, of which we can have, no experience.

They were trying to make a king of him, and they were missing the point so hopelessly. They were expecting him to muster an army in the desert, as Moses did before him, as Mahomet did after him, and achieve an epic of conquest, driving out the Roman invaders from the sacred soil of Palestine—as if that were what Christianity is about! He tries to make them see all that, and the result, at the end of the chapter, is a curious one. "After this, many of his disciples went back to their old ways, and walked no more in his company." Oh, I expect they were very polite about it; they went away saying, "Thank you so much; it has been a very interesting experience." But they went back to their old ways, and walked no more in his company. It is then that he turns to the Twelve, and asks, "Would you too go away?" And Peter—you know it will be Peter—answers for the rest, "Lord, to whom should we go? Thy words are the words of eternal life." He speaks for the rest—for all of them? Our Lord knows better than that; he looks forward to a more dreadful leakage which is to follow: "Have I not chosen all twelve of you? And one of you is a devil." That is for the future, apostasy on the grand scale; here you have only the common or garden lapse of the faint-hearted.

Because our Lord Jesus Christ founded a world-wide Church; because that Church consists of human beings, and is marshalled under the leadership of human beings, it will always be mistaken for the thing that nearly came to exist, all those centuries ago, in the desert country of Palestine; would have come to exist, humanly speaking, if our Lord had not walked away, at dead of night, over the waters of the Lake of Galilee. I mean, a political organization working for its own worldly ends under the nominal leadership of Jesus Christ.

Don't let us make any mistakes about it—that is what

nearly everybody outside the Church thinks we are. They think we are a plot. They put it more politely than that, they call us a pressure-group. But of course that's nonsense; the world is full of pressure-groups; the temperance people are a pressure-group, the sabbath-day observance league is a pressure-group, the Society for the Prevention of Cruelty to Animals is a pressure-group; nobody minds that. No, they think we are a plot; we are out to govern the world. We don't want the world to be run by Russia or by America; we want it run by the Pope instead. When they read the Catholic press, they get the idea more firm in their heads than ever; here is the whole of the week's news set out for you triumphantly or regretfully, according as the Holy Father would or wouldn't have liked it to happen. Well, the Catholic press is not to blame; it can't fill up entirely with headlines about NUNS MEET BABOON ON WAY TO BENEDICTION and so on; they must have an attitude towards the news, and naturally it is a Catholic attitude. But, have you ever tried to persuade a non-Catholic that we aren't a plot? It's awfully difficult. What is more natural than to treat the Catholic religion as if it were simply one among the ideologies?

Do we ourselves treat the Catholic religion as if it were simply one among the ideologies?

I think we do that, ever so little, all the time; we can't help it. Man is a social animal, and he can't help feeling ambitious for the success—for the worldly success—of his own crowd. His own school, his own home town, his own country, his own church, has got to be Number One, openly for all the world to see, or there is a dull discontent at his heart. But remember, in proportion as we encourage that spirit in ourselves, in proportion as we let it affect our attitude and colour our conversation, we are doing religion a mischief. To be more sorry for the Catholic Arabs than for the Mahometan Arabs when they are homeless, to be more sorry for Catholics than for Jews when they go to concentration camps for no fault of their own, is a natural sympathy of ours, but we mustn't let it get *hold* of us. We don't want to be school-tie Christians, more than we can help.

At the back of it all, you see, there's a kind of natural vanity which makes us want to belong to the winning lot. And the thing which happened that day at Capharnaum, when so many of our Lord's followers left him because he told them he wasn't out for worldly success, was prophetic of much that has happened in the history of his Church. There always is, there always has been a penumbra of Christians who are fair-weather Christians, who stick to their religion so long, and only so long, as the going is good. How they flocked into the Church, those people, when the world became Christian under Constantine! How they flock out of the Church, when religion is no longer in vogue, and some newer movement—Protestantism, Nazism, Communism, comes along to claim the allegiance of the crowd-minded!

That early leakage was only a dim foreshadowing of later history. Our Lord said of these people, "No sooner does tribulation or persecution arise than they are scandalized" —that is, they are taken by surprise, they get a nasty jolt; they hadn't bargained for this sort of thing, when they joined the Church. It's not just that they are afraid, they are disillusioned; the proposition doesn't look so good after all. They thought being a Catholic was the latest thing, and it wasn't the latest thing; it hasn't come up to their worldly specifications. Had they ever faith? One hopes not; at least they never seem to have understood what faith meant, what faith involved.

What faith means in this context, St. Paul tells us in the eleventh chapter of his epistle to the Hebrews, that glorious chapter which calls the roll of all the Old Testament heroes, and shows how all of them lived for the hope of something which was going to happen in the future, triumphed, in that hope, over the afflictions of the present. "Faith," the apostle says, "is that which gives substance to our hopes, convinces us of things we cannot see." And it is dead contrary—that is the point I am trying to make—to that human instinct in us which makes us always want to *see results*.

This meditation is about seeing results. We've been talking, so far, about the most vulgar form which that desire can take; the desire which shallow minds have to see the Christian religion, which belongs to eternity, become a fashionable thing and a victorious thing in this limited world of time. So the Jews of our Lord's day wanted to see him at the head of a successful agitation against the Roman invader. So in our own day there are some who are scandalized, get a nasty jolt, when they find that the Catholic faith is execrated over half the globe. We can all see, I hope, that that is a foolish attitude of mind. Our Lord didn't die on a cross to make you and me feel comfortable.

I think Catholics in England are at an advantage in this connexion; we look back on such a long period of persecution, and even since then we have been so carefully kept in place by our neighbours, that we almost take it for granted that the Church will get a raw deal everywhere. On the very rare occasions when I have instructed a convert, I have always devoted the last hour of instructions to a long dissertation, from every point of view, about how beastly it is being a Catholic, and finished up by saying, "Are you sure you still want to be received?" This attitude of holy pessimism makes it easier for our faith to stand up to the shock; we don't expect results because we are so unaccustomed to seeing them.

Why, nowadays they can't even have fighting in Central Africa, they can't even have rioting in South Africa, without killing a nun; and we say vaguely, "Well, I suppose that sort of thing is bound to happen." If anything, the danger is that we won't pray enough for the persecuted, for the prisoners, for the persecutors; we shall take it too much for granted. That won't do; our Lord has told us, in the parable of the Unjust Judge, that we've got to go on and on praying about the persecutions of the Church. The Unjust Judge, if you remember, grants the poor widow redress in the end because he can't have her coming and boring him any longer; in a sort of way we've got to bore Almighty God with our prayers—feel as if we were, anyhow; *we* mustn't get tired of it first. Only, when our prayers are not granted, for what seems to us a very long time, we are not to be scandalized, we are not to be surprised about it. If we could always get cheap and easy results, faith wouldn't come in; and we are to live by faith.

And that, of course, goes for our other prayers as well—

intercessory prayers, I mean. We ask God for a whole lot
of things on behalf of the people we are interested in; health
and happiness and conversion and so on. Here, too, our
instinct is to be impatient for results; here, too, our faith
is exercised, because the results so often don't come. It's
very extraordinary, if you come to think of it, that we
should expect our prayers to be so effective. Once you reflect what God is, and what is the scale of his operations
even within the sphere of this presumably not very important world, it's difficult to see why you or I should expect our prayers to make much more difference than a
school-boy's water-pistol with the Houses of Parliament on
fire. But somehow we forget all that; why do my prayers
make so little difference to Marshal Tito? Here's a perfectly
ordinary lapsed Catholic, surely to goodness it oughtn't to
be very difficult to get the man back to his duties? And yet
my prayers seem to make no difference; the man goes on
just the same. Probably both ways of looking at the thing
are equally deceptive. All I know really is that this obstacle
of Marshal Tito is one fulcrum against which the lever of
my faith is meant to work. Prayer is good for you and me
because it's always prayer in the dark.

I *am* sorry this is such an untidy meditation; but you do,
I hope, see the kind of thing I mean. What I'm trying to say
is that you and I aren't meant to see much in the way of
results. Of course, we do sometimes come across a special
providence or an answer to prayer, just to keep us going.
But to be always asking for results is to show a certain want
of faith. As we look round at the world, we are always finding things, and still more people, to be disappointed in. The

Catholic religion seems to make so much less difference than it ought to. Here is So-and-so, we complain, a boy who goes to a perfectly good Catholic school, why does he never go to Mass (except on Sunday) in the holidays? How is it that the Church collectors manage to spend so much time in the pub, and the Children of Mary never stop talking scandal? Why is it that going to Communion week after week seems to make so little difference in people's lives? We *would* like to see some results.

Well, I'm not sure that it is a really healthy sign when we are given to talking like that; being discontented with other people so often means that we ought to be being discontented with ourselves. But that's another point; what I'm trying to suggest now is, once again, that we are showing a lack of faith. We want to see the pudding proved in the eating, and of course we mustn't expect to. We don't really know what's going on inside other people. We don't know what are the temptations they have to fight; we don't know how much a bad digestion accounts for ill-temper, or mere shyness for what sounds like deliberate rudeness. When I was a seminary professor, we used to meet from time to time and discuss each of the students in turn, trying to figure out whether he would make a good priest. When one of your own penitents came up for discussion, you had to sit quiet and say nothing. And it was extraordinary how little the other people knew, and how wrong the other people could be, when you listened to what they said.

Well, I've left you one loop-hole, haven't I? You mustn't complain when God allows the wicked to triumph, and his own servants to be persecuted; that would be asking to see results. You mustn't complain when your prayers don't get answered; that would be asking to see results. You mustn't complain when your fellow-Catholics appear to be no better than other people; that would be asking to see results. But what about yourself? When you look back over the months which have passed since your last retreat, and reflect what kind of Catholic you still are—or perhaps even have become; surely *there* you are entitled to demand results, and to be disappointed if you don't find any? Well, I wonder. All the time you have been following this meditation, your hair and your nails have been growing; and if God makes these alterations in our bodies without our being conscious of it, are we certain that he isn't doing the same kind of thing with our souls? How do we know that he isn't softening us here, hardening us there, digging deeper at this point, making more room at that, to prepare us for the next test he has in store for us, and we none the wiser? It is such a tiny little surface of our souls that really lies under our observation. When some friend indulges in self-analysis, how wrong they nearly always are! Even we can see it.

No, by all means let us accuse ourselves of having done our best, so often, to thwart the action of God's grace. But have we succeeded in thwarting it? Only he can tell. "I am brought to nothing, I am all ignorance, standing there like a dumb beast before thee"; let us be content to say that, with King David, and leave our Lord to do what he wants with us, down there in the depths which are beyond our knowing.

16 Three Effects of the Passion

OUR LORD spoke from his cross—if the gospels give us a full account of the scene—seven times. And only three of those seven words which cut into the silence of Calvary betray, in our Lord, any consciousness of his human surroundings; only three have any reference to the world of men and women which he was leaving. He prayed for his murderers; he rewarded the confession of the penitent thief with the assurance of Paradise; he assigned his Blessed Mother to the care of that disciple whom, in some special sense, he loved. I don't think it is fanciful if we read, in those three utterances of his, three separate meanings which the Passion has for ourselves.

For ourselves—we cannot be certain that the Passion had no other, more intimate meaning, in which the salvation of mankind was not directly concerned. We know that the saints, built, surely, in a different mould from ourselves, have desired, have prayed for, martyrdom; we know that suffering, for them, was not a nightmare to be avoided, but a privilege to be sued for, almost a right to be claimed. And it may be that in the inner life of Jesus Christ, which is revealed to us in the gospels only by stray hints and confidential asides, Calvary had something of the same significance. It may have been, quite apart from anything else, the only full expression, the only appropriate consummation, of a love like his. All that, we don't know; divine revelation only tells us about what Jesus Christ did and was for our sakes, *propter nos homines;* that is the furthest point we can expect to reach in the theology of the Passion.

(i)

"Father, forgive them; they do not know what it is they are doing." When our Lord told his disciples beforehand how he was to suffer, he included one curious item in the crime-sheet for which the chief priests would make themselves responsible; "they will hand him over to the Gentiles." Why was that important? Why should it add to the tragedy of the situation, to the heinousness of their offence? Was it that they tried to shelve their responsibility for putting the Son of God to death, by making it appear as if their part in the whole business was a merely formal, a merely judicial one—it was the Gentiles, not his own people, who killed him?

St. Augustine does write as if the Jews had been guilty of such hypocrisy. "That, to be sure, was in their minds when they handed him over to Pilate's jurisdiction; his death should not be laid at their door. Kill him yourselves, was Pilate's word to them; but they had an answer to that, We have no power to put any man to death. The guilt of their crime should rest on another man's shoulders." But St. Augustine, in that splendid passage which we read in the nocturne of Tenebrae, was more concerned to interpret the psalms than to expound the gospels. And if you read the gospels, I think it is hard to make out that the Jews meant to put the blame on Pilate. When he disclaimed responsibility, they cried out willingly enough, "His blood be upon us, and upon our children." No, the Gentiles come into the picture more subtly than that.

The point, surely, is an ironical one—it was entirely a domestic affair, the business of the Jewish people and nobody else, this business of rejecting and murdering the Messiah. He was *their* Saviour; nothing had been said yet about his being the Saviour of the world. Theirs, to welcome him if they would, and inherit the promises made long ago to their fathers. Theirs, to reject him if they would, and fulfil every gloomy foreboding of the prophets in doing so; but at least let it be their own act, condemning him to a shameful death! At least let them be his judges, his executioners, as they were judges and executioners when St. Stephen was martyred, only a short time afterwards. But no, they would be content to march up and down, enjoying the spectacle, while a Roman governor put their Prisoner to death, and placarded his cross with a legend that was an open insult to the Jewish people!

Here they are, then, an execution-squad of Roman soldiers, carrying out their orders without much zest, but trying to get a little amusement out of it as they go along; dressing up their Prisoner so as to make him look a fool, seeing if they can't sting him up with a blow here and there, and so on. Roman soldiers, we call them, but we only know that they served under the Roman colours; they may have come from any distant province. They don't know anything about him, except that he is some kind of visionary; a bit of a magician, by all accounts. They don't treat him any worse than they would treat any other prisoner who was helpless in their hands, any other mild sort of person who didn't show fight. That is the horrible thing about human nature—human nature fallen back in the direction of the beast—that weakness, helplessness, which make us pity a human being on paper, are so apt to make worse brutes of us when we come face to face with them; you find that everywhere, from bullying at school right up to the worst horrors of the concentration-camp. They are not, in intention, persecuting the Saviour of the world. They are only baiting a Jew.

"Father, forgive them; they don't know what it is they are doing"—was that said in extenuation of their fault? Perhaps, and yet it was but a poor extenuation of it; even if our Lord had been what they thought he was, he might have claimed their pity. It is possible to give a different twist to the sentence; the ignorance of our Lord's persecutors is perhaps meant to explain, not why they deserve, but why they need forgiveness. If they only knew what they were doing, these soldiers are instruments in the hand of Providence, securing the redemption of the world by the sacrifice of a Divine Victim. But they don't know all that; they are just bullies, taking the first opportunity that comes to hand for indulging their instinct of cruelty—therefore, Father, forgive them. The effect, in any case, is the same; the point is that there is no question of theology here, because the people with whom our Lord is concerned are not his fellow-countrymen; know nothing about the prophets or about the hope of Israel. To them, he is simply a man; and for them, simply as a Man, he prays, to give us men an example. We are to forgive our enemies; find excuses for them, as best we can; we are to pray for them, meaning it.

What a trite, what an obvious moral! Yes, but not an easy one. How often, when you thought you had been badly treated, have you forgiven? Oh, one forgets; time passes, and we come to see our grievances in a juster perspective. But how often have you, with the example of Jesus Christ before you, actually managed to forgive an injury; to see the other person's point of view, and make allowances for it; to be able to think of that person, when a week or so has passed, without a rebellious tide of anger surging up in your heart? Well, you say, one's feelings are so difficult to control. True, but how often have you managed to stifle down the uncharitable comment which occurred to you when that person's name was mentioned in company? How often have you devised some little mark of attention, even if it was only sending a picture postcard from the sea-side, to make that person feel that you didn't bear any malice? Not often, I suspect. And yet that was what Jesus Christ was meaning you to do, when the nails went in.

Upon my word, I think it is the most frightening and the most depressing thing about the frightening and depressing times we live in, that the obvious moral of the cross should be so much misunderstood. I mean, we have seen so much heroism in our time; so much high courage in resisting tyranny, so much patience under persecution; and people will talk as if all this self-sacrificing idealism—not all with one inspiration, not all under one banner—were proof that the spirit of Christ crucified still reigns among us; his splendid indifference to popularity, his contempt of worldly values. But all that, although of course it comes out in the story of the Passion, is not specifically Christian; the Stoics were preaching and practising those virtues in our Lord's time, just as they are practised in our own. But Jesus Christ taught us, tried to teach us, forgiveness. And do we forgive?

(ii)

It is one thing to pray for your neighbour's forgiveness, as any man may do, as all men ought to do. It is another thing to grant forgiveness; that belongs only to God, or to the Church acting in his name. And when our Lord speaks next, he speaks as God. Oh, he does not use a formula of absolution, any more than the thief makes a formal confession; there are moments, one must suppose, at which formalities go by the board. The thief has matched his own life with the life of the innocent stranger who hangs beside him, and found grace to see it as the sinful thing it is. "And we justly enough; we receive no more than the due reward of our deeds; but this man has done nothing amiss." Not like the professional lag, you see, complaining of the bad luck he's had, how the police bullied him, how the judge was hard on him; no, "justly enough." Not like you and me, for that matter, on Saturday nights, when we have to dig out

our sins; "of course, there were rather special circumstances
. . . I did try, Father. . . . Father, I think perhaps I ought
to explain. . . ."—no, "justly enough." The cross has got
him thinking straight; and, besides, he feels the stupendous
contrast between his record and the record of his fellow-
Sufferer, so unselfish, so unresisting, so unassuming, "this
man has done nothing amiss." And with the sense of contrast comes, he doesn't know how, a sense of confidence;
how can this *not* be the Christ? How can you doubt that
a kingdom awaits him? Some time, somewhere; of course
I shan't be around, but, Sir, when you come into your
kingdom, don't forget a poor man that spoke up for you.

Only, you see, he's got it wrong; the contrast wasn't the
point—at least, not all the point. Jesus Christ didn't come
into the world and suffer merely so as to make us ashamed
when we saw ourselves so unlike him. The innocence and
the guilt were not just contrasted, they were somehow
complementary; to be hanging there at the side of the Innocent wasn't the wrong place for the guilty man, it was
just the right place. The clash of colours was not a discord,
after all, it was a daring harmony. The penitent is shriven;
but how to explain all that to him, here and now; here, on
a cross, now, with death just round the corner? Enough to
set his mind at rest; "I promise thee, this day thou shalt be
with me in Paradise." This day (cries Bossuet), what
promptitude! With me, what company! In Paradise, what
repose!

No, our Lord won't bother the poor, aching head of his
fellow-sufferer with theology; the sentence of absolution
shall be as informal as the act of contrition. He is content

to promise that, at their journey's end, they will still be together, and he will be saying, "Please let this person in; he is a friend of mine." But behind all that, as we know, lies the curiously simple but curiously puzzling doctrine of the Atonement. Curiously simple—a child can understand, seems to understand instinctively, the idea of "making it up" to somebody. A mother's feelings have been injured by some piece of rudeness or disobedience; it is not enough to say you are sorry—there must be some token present made, some little attention paid that is out of the common, to make amends for the fault. That our sins, on an infinitely greater scale, are an offence against God, we can see clearly enough; and at the same time we can see all too clearly that no reparation we could offer is sufficient reparation; we cannot be content with nursery make-believe. The debt which we owe to the outraged majesty of God cannot be honoured in our worthless human currency. If satisfaction is to be made, at least if satisfaction is to be made in full, only infinite worth in the Victim can atone for the infinite malice of the affront.

All *that* we can understand easily enough; and yet, what difficulties it raises if we try to think out the implications of it! That the God who so loved us could yet deal so strictly with us; that his justice should demand what only his mercy can provide! And again, that the sacrifice our Lord made should weigh in the balance against sins that were not his own; that the occupant of *this* cross should win his Paradise through the merits of that other—what human analogy can we find for such a transaction which really covers it? All that mystery we have to accept; rub out the doctrine of the Atonement from your theology, and you have altered the whole emphasis, the whole basis of the Christian religion.

> "The dying thief rejoiced to see
> That fountain in his day;
> And there may I, as vile as he,
> Wash all my sins away."

There can be no Christian death-bed which does not repose in that confidence.

(iii)

At the same time, I think it would be a great mistake to go away from our meditation on the Passion thinking that we have exhausted the whole meaning of it, when we have allowed it to remind us of our Lord's Atonement. Because there is a mystical significance in the Passion which is, you may say, something even more familiar, and perhaps even more central, in the thought of St. Paul. The interminable controversies that have raged about the doctrine of grace have given us a sort of feeling that St. Paul was constantly thinking and writing about the Atonement, that and nothing else. But as a matter of fact, if you will read St. Paul's epistles as a whole, not concentrating all your attention on one or two chapters in the Galatians and the Romans, you will find that your impression is quite wrong. What is uppermost in St. Paul's mind when he thinks about the Death of Jesus Christ is not so much that he died for us,

although of course St. Paul believes that just like any other
Christian. The exciting thing to St. Paul's mind is not so
much that Christ died for us, as that we died with and in
Christ. And that brings us on (though the connexion may
seem obscure) to the third utterance we said we were going
to talk about—our Lord's words of encouragement to St.
John and to his Blessed Mother—"Behold thy son, Behold
thy mother."

It puzzles us at first sight, to know why our Lady had
to be provided with a new home. There is no doubt, I
think, that that is the sense of the Greek; St. John actually
behaved to her as a son would have, as her own Son surely
would have, had it been his destiny to live. For some reason,
those kinsmen of hers, who are so often mentioned in the
gospels, were not to have the privilege of supporting the
Mother of God in her widowhood. But all that was a matter
of mere history; and here, as nearly always in St. John's
Gospel, you have the instinct that he meant you to penetrate beneath the surface and not be content with mere
history; there is a mystical meaning that underlies it.

It was, no doubt, a practical arrangement that our Lord
was making, but it was something more than a practical
arrangement; it was the sacramental expression of a truth
he was wanting to teach us, there on the cross. And this
truth was, surely, that after his death nothing could be the
same; it opened up a new set of relationships, to supersede
the old. Hitherto, men had been grouped together by bonds
of family or of race; now a new, supernatural relationship
was coming into the world—the Church, his own mystical
Body; the kingdom in which his followers were to be

grouped, the sphere in which his followers were to move, thenceforward. A kingdom of grace, not abolishing indeed but overshadowing all earthly loyalties.

"See, here is thy son . . . here is thy mother"—the death-pangs of our Redeemer were to be the birth-pangs of a redeemed world. All of us, who are incorporated into Christ by baptism, undergo a mystical death in union with him; we die to nature, and come to birth in a world of grace. You and I commonly think of baptism as a process of cleansing, that washes our sins away from us; St. Paul writes of it, much more often, as a process of dying, which buries us away from our sins. The guilt of our sins lies behind us, because we are new people, we are dead to all that. But it is not only the guilt, it is the power of our sins that we have left behind us; the grip is relaxed. Children of that supernatural family which came into being when our Lady and St. John found their new kinship, we have shaken off all the ties by which our old nature bound us, sin included.

This doctrine of the new birth can be, and sometimes has been, dangerously exploited. Although we belong to the kingdom of grace, our fallen nature has not been wholly bred out of us; our perfection is something in the making, not something already achieved. But I think we Catholics are too apt to forget this third significance of the Passion; when we look at the crucifix, we say to ourselves, "What an example to follow!"; we say to ourselves, "He died to redeem me"; we forget to add, "when he died, I died too." The world is crucified to me, and I to the world; I am dead, and my life is hidden with Christ in God—if we tried to remember that, if we let our meditation on Calvary be soaked in that conviction, I think our efforts to live as Jesus Christ wants us to live would be less fumbling, less half-hearted. He wants us to live as if we were dead; for we *are* dead now; crucified to the world, and buried with him.

17 Death

THERE is an old saying in our language, at least three hundred years old, that "nine tailors make a man"; and, for no very obvious reason, the members of a hard-working profession have been stigmatized in our literature as lacking in personal courage. But it is an open question whether the old saying means anything of the kind. Those people who are learned about the ringing of church bells assure us that "tailor" is a mispronunciation of the word "teller"; and the tellers are the preliminary strokes of the bell which announced a death in the parish before you went on to the "tolling" proper, that is, ringing one stroke for each year of the deceased person's age. In some parishes—ours, for instance—you rang three of these tellers for a man, two for a woman, one for a child. But elsewhere you rang nine times for a man, six times for a woman; and that is how the ringers came to say to one another, "nine tailors make a man"; they weren't referring to the people who make our clothes at all.

So I thought we would divide up our meditation on death into nine points, one for each stroke of the bell. There is such a lot to be said about death, and it is all very obvious. But we ought, I suppose, to recall it to our minds occasionally, especially on the occasion of a retreat. And if you ever find yourself in a country parish where the old customs are observed, those traditional nine strokes will remind you of this retreat.

ONE;—death means rest; rest from hard work, from acute pain, from all the regrets and solicitudes which haunt the mind. That moral is clear enough, even to the mind of a pagan who does not believe in a future life.

> "Duncan is in his grave;
> After life's fitful fever he sleeps well;
> Treason has done his worst: nor steel, nor poison,
> Malice domestic, foreign levy, nothing
> Can touch him further."

To be sure, all this is rather a negative kind of consolation. When we talk about resting after a set of tennis or a parish bazaar, we mean a positive feeling of contentment; of lying back and putting our feet up and comparing today with yesterday. The pagan looks forward to nothing of that kind; only to a total absence of sensation in which the unpleasant sensations have gone with the others. We too, believing Christians, talk of the dead as being "at rest"; but evidently in a different sense, or why do we ask God, in the same breath, to grant them rest and peace, as something still needed beyond the grave? For us, the doctrine of Purgatory casts its shadow over the future; we dare not tell ourselves that we have finished with discomfort and weariness and the sense of frustration when the soul has left the body; all that—we have good reason to suppose—still waits to be experienced.

And yet, if you come to think of it, the holy souls in Purgatory are already at rest, in a sense almost unimaginable to us. The tension is relaxed; the tension, I mean, which is set up even in a very mediocre Christian life by the mere fact that we are trying to serve a God we cannot see, in the hope of a future life for which we have no evidence beyond hearsay. Our probation-time will be over, when we reach Purgatory, and that gnawing sense of anxiety which faith brings with it will already be replaced by a tangible experience of the supernatural world—at least the fringes of it. As a man who has committed himself, on a friend's authority, to an unknown shortcut on his homeward journey feels his mind at rest when he begins to sight the familiar landmarks, so we shall experience rest of mind, please God, when we wake up after death to find that we are not dead.

TWO;—death strips us; puts away the toys we cherished. Shrouds have no pockets; a cheque signed by a dead man is no longer honoured. We are still indebted, as you see, to the copy-books; philosophers and poets were talking about this long before Christianity came into the world to confuse our speculations. We could always see that the miser was a pitiable creature; that is why we called him the miser; we could always see that the man who built a house too big for his needs was a fool; that is why our English landscape is still dotted with piles of masonry that are nicknamed So-and-so's Folly.

And when our Lord told his disciples the parable of the Rich Fool he was, for once, talking good heathen morality; you did not need to be a disciple of his to see that death can make our human planning for the future look silly. Today, we don't hoard up money, because we are afraid of devaluation; we don't build big houses, because we know we couldn't find anybody to sweep the passages. But we men are incurably prehensile; Easter after Easter St. Paul warns us not to set our affections on things on the earth, and we always do. We are possessive about our friendships, about our books and furniture, about the petty privileges which come to us as the result of seniority or rank; nor does old age make us less tenacious of them. We behave as if the things of this world, ours only on a lease-lend basis, were the real treasures worth having. And in all that, ever so slightly, we try to cushion ourselves against the thought of eternity. Because of that, this second stroke of the passing-bell is worth listening to, for Christians even more than for other people.

THREE;—Death levels us; the nine tailors only assure us that a *man* is dead; they do not tell us whether it is the squire or the village idiot. The copy-books again:

"Death lays his icy hand on kings.
　Sceptre and Crown
　Must tumble down,
And in the dust be equal made
With the poor crooked scythe and spade."

Well, here again times have changed; we live in a world from which privilege has disappeared, or at any rate we don't talk about it. But you can't really have equality in this world; some of us are cleverer than others, some of us

more artistic, some of us more efficient, some of us more
socially attractive than others, and at the back of our minds
we are conscious of it. We like to go where we are appreciated, and to make friends whose gifts will play up to ours;
to establish a little world of our own, from which the general public is excluded. No great harm is done; but to that
extent the thought of death will be an uncomfortable one.
The list of priorities in the next world will obviously be
so different from ours. . . . It will do no harm if the thought
of death sometimes makes us take more trouble about the
people who, in this world, get counted out and left in a
corner.

FOUR;—death may come at any time; we can't even be
sure that we shall be given a minute or two to prepare ourselves for it. At this point we leave the copy-books behind;
because although the fact is painfully obvious, there is no
reason why a pagan, with no belief in a future life, should
mind dying suddenly. It will give him no opportunity to
alter his will, but that's about all there is to it. For the
Christian, the threat of sudden death means something quite
different. All those warnings our Lord gave us about the
suddenness of the Last Judgement apply with equal force,
we feel, to the last moment of our lives. What we are then,
in the sight of God, we shall be to all eternity.

Yes, it's a Christian moral, this one; but something tells
us that it's Christianity at a rather low level. Isn't there
something rather calculating, rather ungenerous, about the
Christian who looks both ways before he crosses the street
going to confession, and doesn't bother on the way back?

Well, of course, there is; but then you have got to remember that a retreat, like a parish mission, was originally meant to do good to people who were living very worldly lives and had almost forgotten to think about eternity. No doubt when we were at school, if we got a retreat of the old-fashioned, hard-baked kind, this business of sudden death was rather over-stressed; you got the impression that Divine Providence was always lying in wait for sinners and catching them out when they weren't looking. This was, we feel now, an appeal to the less generous side of us; it played too much on our fears. But it *is* true that in the liturgy we ask to be delivered from sudden and unforeseen death. And even if we have lived for years under the shadow of the sacraments, it would savour of presumption, I think, to *pray* that we might die suddenly. To be scrupulous about sins which we have confessed long ago is mere waste of spiritual energy. But to have a little time, even if it's only an hour or two, to polish up our consciences and make them shine a little clearer against our judgement—that is a natural thing to ask for, if it should be God's will.

FIVE;—death must come some time; and therefore a limit is set to all our human activities; we must start soon if we want to get anything finished. Clearly you needn't be a Christian, needn't be under the influence of religion in any way, to come up against that fact. *Ars longa, vita brevis;* the human animal is always setting itself tasks to do, and always in a competitive spirit; take your front-garden in hand, and before the year is out you will be determined to make it the best garden in the neighbourhood. With that combination of restlessness and vanity in us, we usually, as the saying goes, bite off more than we can chew; so that when death comes it leaves untidy edges; there are still ugly gaps in the stamp album, the epic has to be published post-humously.

But of course, if we look squarely at the facts, there is no tragedy, from the merely pagan point of view, about this incompleteness in our human efforts. If death means extinction, the unfinished task robs nobody except posterity, and posterity cares very little one way or the other. Men work for fame; and the hope of fame is not a bad thing to work for; but once you are dead, it can make no difference whether you are famous or not. What matter whether you arrived, so long as you travelled hopefully?

But for us Christian people the shortness of life brings a real responsibility, and a real anxiety. God has a job for you to do in this world; probably a very modest one—to overcome such and such weaknesses in your own nature, to be of use to such and such souls with whom he brings you into contact, to make your tiny contribution to the success of such and such a movement. That is your talent, given you to trade with, not to bury it underground. And the span of life he has allotted you is long enough to let you get that job well and truly done, as long as you are quick off the mark. But are you quick off the mark? Few of us are. It's a remarkable thing, how many of the canonized saints died before the age of forty.

SIX;—death is the moment of decision; is the tape at the end of the race, the cease-fire at the end of the battle. Or, if you will, it is the relieving of the guard; the point is, in any case, that until death comes we must always be on our toes; there is no excuse for relaxation of effort. That is why we must pray, always, for the grace of perseverance. Our heathen friend, to be sure, will make nothing of all that; why should there be no relaxation of effort? Surely that is just what old age is meant for, to be a slow running-down of the engines before they shut off. (I was trying to show you, when I talked to you about perseverance, what a temptation there is for us Christians, as life goes on, to fall into that essentially heathen attitude. When our natural powers fail, we make it an excuse for relaxing supernatural effort.) But we Christians are engaged to work while it is day; there is no question of calling it a day, and knocking off. We mustn't underestimate the force of the temptation; the weakening of our natural powers, the sameness of things, the feeling that we've nobody now depending on us much —can't I afford to let things go a little? But there is no letting things go, until that final act by which we let our souls go into the keeping of our heavenly Father.

SEVEN;—death is a painful experience, and we shall be better able to square up to it if we have at least a bowing acquaintance with pain. That is, in part, the meaning of mortification. Asceticism is not a merely Christian affair; the undergraduate who goes into training to win a race or a match is, to that extent, an ascetic. But he is training for life; Christian asceticism trains us for death. Oh, mortification has plenty of other grounds to recommend it; we want to unite ourselves with the sufferings of our Lord; to make satisfaction for our own sins and for the sins of others; to anticipate our Purgatory, and so on.

But this mortification, this doing of ourselves to death, which is only mentioned among Christians and perhaps even among them not often enough—it has a nearer and a more practical aim, to give us an apprenticeship in that discipline of suffering which generally precedes and accompanies our departure from the world. It is meant to produce in us a habit of resignation; and therefore it needn't mean, though it does sometimes mean, voluntarily inflicting pain or discomfort on ourselves. If we have learned to put up with the minor inconveniences of life without pitying ourselves, or asking for pity, without excusing ourselves from ordinary duties, or forgetting the claims of charity towards others, we have already taken a step, and a big step, on the road of mortification. And when death comes, it will not take us altogether by surprise. It is something we had bargained for.

EIGHT;—death is the consummation of sacrifice. Our whole life, as Christians, has got to be a sacrifice continually offered to God; we are his creatures, depending on him from moment to moment for our very existence, and it is our business to attest the consciousness of that fact by remitting to him the control of our destinies, trusting him to know better than we know what is best for us. And in resigning ourselves to death at a moment of his choosing we seal and deliver that deed of gift by which we want to belong to him.

That is why suicide is such a terrible sin. The heathen, finding himself unable to live his own life, has at least the miserable option—or so he thinks—of dying his own death. That is, in fact, to rob God of the obedience owed to him just where it matters most. For we, God's creatures, have no more splendid opportunity of acknowledging our creatureliness than when we submit to death. Of our own nature, we are nothing; and if he ceased to will our existence, we should lapse into the nothing from which we came. It is his will that our souls should survive after death; death, therefore, is not extinction, but it is, you may say, a dress-rehearsal of extinction; the separation of the soul from the body which has always been its natural means of self-expression feels like ceasing to exist. We cannot, as our Lord did, lay down life by a mere act of the will. But we can turn death into a willed act by accepting it, and the manner and the moment of it. Shall we be able to do that, on our death-beds? Most people die, to all outward appearance, in a state of unconsciousness. Let us make, then, that act of acceptance beforehand; while life is still strong in us; and not least when we go into retreat.

NINE;—death is a bursting into life; the manifestation of that risen life which now obscurely labours in us. We are always forgetting that so long as we are in a state of grace we Christians are living with the life of Jesus Christ; and if we die in a state of grace it is with that life, not with the common animal life by which we draw breath here, that we shall find ourselves living. The pagans, when they dared to hope for a life beyond the grave and tried to picture it, could only picture it as a continuation of their earthly experience; so you find the heroes in Virgil's *Aeneid* spending their time in Elysium—how do you think? Grooming their horses. I suppose there would be a kind of consolation in it, if some angel should reveal to us that we were going to spend eternity washing down the car.

But, you see, that is not the sort of thing we mean by eternal life. We mean something which is already here, please God, within us, but betrays no sensible sign of its presence. After death we shall have the experience of living with it. Not that it will find its full scope until we reach heaven; while our Purgatory lasts, it cannot, one imagines, function freely or naturally. Not the flower yet, but already the bud; that life will be unfolding itself in us as the buds unfold in spring-time; the fires of Purgatory will be only the sun that ripens it, leaf by leaf, petal by petal, with delicate adumbrations of the glory that awaits us. The darkness of that night will be lit up, however faintly, by the lurid clouds of morning.

18 Eternity

We have spoken of death; whether, in times of retreat, we ought to look beyond that and consider what happens to us in eternity, is a thing I could never be certain about. I am going to try and say something, now, about heaven and hell, but not with the purpose of producing any lively effect on your imaginations, as one is ordinarily expected to do. I only want to straighten out my own ideas, and I hope yours, about the kind of shadow which eternity ought to cast over our lives here upon earth. There is to be no overstrained piety on the one hand, no horrors on the other. But it will just serve to remind us that the life which awaits us beyond death is what really matters, and that anything which happens to us in this life is only of importance when you look at it in the light of eternity; if we don't do that much, we shall get the whole perspective of the Christian religion wrong.

Heaven and hell—we find it difficult to imagine either of them; but let us remember in passing that the reason for this deficiency in us is not the same in either case. Heaven stands by itself; St. Paul tells us that "no eye has seen, no ear has heard, no human heart has conceived the welcome God has prepared for those who love him." Nothing of that kind is said about the destiny of those who hate him. Nothing leads us to suppose that if we fall away from grace, and die in that unhappy condition, we shall develop a special susceptibility to pain, whether of mind or body; the sense of abandonment we feel will be the same as the sense of abandonment we feel here—only it will be all-embracing, only it will be everlasting. And the suffering which afflicts us from the outside will come to us through those same gateways of sense by which, here on earth, suffering penetrates into the fastnesses of the inner life. Whereas heaven, in the very nature of the case, is something which we can't possibly imagine; we have to make up stories about harps and crowns and palm-branches and things in the hope of cheating ourselves into the idea that we *can* imagine what it's like; and of course we don't succeed. We must go into all that more fully later on; all I want to point out at the moment is that we mustn't think of heaven and hell as entirely symmetrical, like two china dogs one on each side of the mantelpiece.

The *Imitation of Christ* says somewhere that the trouble about these things—I mean, about the realities of the supernatural world—is not so much that we don't believe in them as that they don't penetrate into our hearts; they don't exercise as much influence on our conduct, or even on our way of looking at things, as they ought to and as we should expect them to.

May I give you a very undignified comparison? You are sitting out of doors somewhere with a party of friends, and one of them gets up and says, "Do you mind? I want to take a photograph." Instinctively, you begin to put your hat straight, or tidy your hair; and the proceeding doesn't really argue any great vanity in you. The point is that this moment is going to be perpetuated; your appearance at this moment is going to be put on record; people will examine the photograph and think that that's what you look like. Probably they will only be passport officials, and it doesn't really matter much; but for all that—no, it is not really vanity, you aren't trying to look your best, but you don't want to look a fright, that's all.

Well, it is a simple parable; we Christians, who know that an eternity lies ahead of us, are (so to speak) facing up to the camera at every moment of our lives. Most of all, to be sure, at the last moment of our lives; the posture in which death finds us will be our posture in eternity. But we can't bank on that last moment, which is so uncertain; at every moment we are weaving the tapestry of our fate; this letter, which you are writing in a great hurry so as not to miss the post, may be the turning-point of a life-time for you, or for the person to whom it is addressed—what a dreadful responsibility! How is it that we live so carelessly, act so impetuously, when so much depends on it, when heaven and hell lie at the end of the thread?

I suppose that if a candid atheist from some distant country were suddenly introduced to contemporary life, he would have a right to be puzzled about it all. "Here are certain people," he would say to himself, "who think that when they die they will be snuffed out like a candle; here are other people, who think that once they are dead they will survive unendingly, in utter happiness or in utter misery, and that their day-to-day actions will make all the difference. How curious that these two classes of people seem to live in exactly the same way, except at eleven o'clock on Sunday morning! They talk in very much the same way, they act in very much the same way, and yet in theory the mainspring of their lives is wholly different! How is it, for example, that people who can look over the edge of this world into the next, and realize what solemn issues are at stake, can sit here chatting and laughing like this; nay, even making jokes to one another about heaven and hell—what can be the matter with them?"

Well, of course all that is going too far. For one thing, most of us have to live our lives in mixed society, rubbing up against people who don't see things as we do, and we all have the instinct—I think it is a right instinct—that we should do harm instead of good if we were obviously trying to come the Christian the whole time. In point of fact, some of the holiest people I have ever known (I can think of several at this moment) were hardly ever without a smile on their lips. And, quite apart from the effect on other people, I don't think it would have a very good effect on ourselves, it would tend to make us priggish and perhaps scrupulous, if we were always thinking about our heavenly crown, or always sniffing brimstone. But all the same I can never read that passage in the *Imitation* without an uneasy feeling that it means me; "these things don't penetrate into our hearts." Why don't they penetrate?

Well, as we were saying just now, it isn't really difficult to see why heaven doesn't get across to us. The happiness of heaven isn't meant to satisfy the needs of our nature; it's an extra, something in the ordinary way quite beyond our reach, so that our nature has to be elevated beyond itself before it can learn to appreciate the flavours of that sublime experience. It's quite true, our nature is in fact elevated already, by the gift of sanctifying grace; but that change has taken place deep down at the roots of it, far below the level of observation. On the surface, even when we are in a state of grace, our nature is what it always was, has the same gross needs and aspirations; if you went to heaven just as you are, you wouldn't appreciate the happiness of heaven any more than a dog would appreciate Shakespeare. And I think if we would be honest with ourselves we feel rather the same about heaven as we have sometimes felt before now about an invitation to a party or a foreign tour or something of that kind—we know we shall enjoy it when we get there, but we can't, here and now, indulge in those pleasures of anticipation which might be expected of us.

In fact, we sometimes wonder, "If I were given the choice between living on and on in this manifestly imperfect world, which is nevertheless so familiar to me, or of being transplanted to that heaven which is so perfect but so unfamiliar, which would I choose?" Fortunately, we are not being given any option about it; God will send his carriage for us at his own time, and his royal summons cannot be disobeyed.

With hell, as we were saying, it is quite different; we shall not need to be elevated into any different condition of being in order to feel the pains of hell. But hell, too, doesn't really get across to us; why is that? I think the cause is, at the roots of it, a psychological one; we don't want hell to hap-

pen and therefore we run away from the thought of it; not
by any conscious process in our minds, but by some much
stronger urge at the back of our minds, we try to pretend
it isn't there. And at first sight it looks as if there was an
obvious remedy for that; we ought to meditate more about
hell—that, surely, is what meditation is meant for, to overcome these weaknesses of the imagination.

Well, if you can do that, and find that it is really useful—
find that you do become less proud and less irritable and
less spiteful as the result of it, by all means go in for that
sort of thing; you have all the books on your side. But, you
know, I think with a great many of us that method just
doesn't work. We try to feel the pains of hell, we try to
plunge ourselves into the dreadful desolation of hell, and
what happens? It only makes a great bruise on the mind,
half fatigue and half distaste, as the result of this head-on
collision with nature; we don't feel freshly armed for the
fight against our temptations, only sullen and depressed.

What are we going to do about it then? Obviously we
have got to do something about it; absurd to suppose that
heaven and hell, which feature so largely in the scheme of
Christian theology, are meant to be tucked away at the back
of our minds and forgotten. I think I would say this about
heaven; that we ought to recall the thought of it deliberately to our minds on certain occasions, when it will use-
fully form a supernatural background for our day-to-day
experience.

Do I mean by that, that when we are feeling particularly
depressed we ought to cheer ourselves up by saying: "It
doesn't matter; this sort of thing doesn't go on for long. I
shall die and go to heaven, and in heaven there won't be

any toothaches or any irritating letters to answer or any east winds or any spiteful remarks"? I don't mean that, though you do get a good deal of that in Christian literature, especially in hymns; those hymns about "Jerusalem, my happy home" and "O Paradise, O Paradise, 'Tis weary waiting here." But then you have got to remember that people do make up poetry chiefly in moments of depression. "Jerusalem, my happy home" was written by a priest in prison; so no wonder he talked about there being no spiders or dust in heaven. And Father Faber, a great man if ever there was one, suffered from almost continuous headaches, so you wouldn't expect him to take this world very cheerfully. But for you and me, I think it's best not to forget about heaven till we are in a really despondent mood, and then dig out the thought of it in an effort to cheer ourselves up. Partly because it isn't really a great compliment to heaven to compare it only with our worst times on earth; and partly because it feels rather like wish-thinking, and makes our pious phrases about the future life ring rather hollow.

No, what I would suggest is that in our times of great happiness, and especially when we have an all-over sense of peace and contentment without (very often) being quite able to account for it, we should let our minds fall back on the thought of heaven and reflect that heaven is something better and something fuller than this. A sunset or a concert which carries us away out of ourselves; or perhaps—for as we get older most of our happiness is reflected from the happiness of other people—when we go to a wedding or watch children at play, *then* we should call heaven to mind, and let our mood of happiness fan out into eternity.

We don't want our happiness to be a mere mood, but a

settled condition; we don't want it to be just ours, we want
to share it with everybody—so we picture it as part of those
heavenly joys which we shall share one day, please God,
with those whom we loved on earth, with the saints who are
bathed in it, glowing with it, according to the more perfect
measure of their receptivity. No, don't let us try to imagine
heaven; we shall get nowhere. Let us only try to see our
present happiness—a mere slice of experience, outlined for
us by contrast with the dull level of ordinary life—against
a background of essential happiness to which, somehow, it
belongs.

And about hell? That's not so easy. I suppose the normal
assumption is that if we never think about it at any other
time, we ought to think about hell when we are confronted
by some grave temptation; we shall sit down in a cool hour
and balance the considerations one against another—some
momentary pleasure, some temporary advantage, put in the
scales against eternal misery. I wonder if that really happens? I mean, temptation has a way of sweeping us off our
feet, so that we are not capable of sitting down and thinking the thing out calmly; the hell-motive, if it comes into
our calculations at all, is not weighed and found wanting;
it is pushed away into the back of the mind, buried away
under a mass of qualifications and excuses.

Don't misunderstand me; I think it probably is true that
the thought of hell at the back of our minds does help to
preserve us from grave sin, perhaps oftener than we know.
But the question I am considering now is something different. When ought we, more especially, to keep the thought
of hell in the forefront of our minds? It is a thought from

which we all tend to run away, and therefore we tell ourselves that we do best to store it up, keep it in reserve, as
a kind of iron ration that will stand us in good stead when
we are up against some really grave temptation, which will
call upon us for heroic resolve. And, as I say, I think that
is doubtful wisdom. Because we may find that that is just
the moment when the thought of hell will not be there to
deter us. Passion has a way of obscuring reason, yes, and
faith itself; we shall be in danger of pushing away the un-
welcome consideration as a mere scruple, a child's fairy-tale.

I wonder if we oughtn't to think of hell, more than we
do, in connexion with our ordinary, dreary, Saturday-after-
Saturday sins? Not that they deserve hell; oh no, they are
venial sins all right. But the point of hell isn't simply that it's
the punishment of our sins; it's also, in a sense, the continuation of our sins; what really makes hell so unpleasant
is what makes our sins so unpleasant—the setting up of
wrong standards, the clinging to oneself and one's own
point of view, the want of submissiveness, the want of
peace, the want of love. Going to hell is going to a place
where all the people, not just some people, all the time, not
just some of the time, are trying to assert themselves and
hating one another.

If you remember, St. James, when he is discussing sins
of the tongue, says that the tongue is "a fire . . . catching
fire itself from hell." He thinks of hell as a great volcano,
still (as far as we are concerned) mercifully dormant, but
shooting up jets of molten lava which come out in your
conversation and mine. You know how people with a pro-
fane habit of speech will tell you that the atmosphere in

the room they've just come from was as hot as hell; how, when you are travelling in the Underground at rush hour, being told to Hurry-along-there-please when you can't even move, you find yourself wondering whether hell will be rather like this. But of course, when we use language like that we are just making guesses about the unknown. It would be far more to the point if we said that the conversation in the room we have just left was as uncharitable as hell; if we wondered whether hell would be like this after an hour spent in indulging our feelings of hatred against somebody we dislike. What makes hell oppressive isn't the want of air, it's the want of divine grace.

Those are the suggestions I would make, proposed with some diffidence, because we are not all built alike. I suggest that we are meant to think about heaven, not so much when we are down in the mouth, as when some feeling of earthly contentment creates in us a longing for wider horizons. I suggest that we are meant to think about hell, not so much when we are suddenly assaulted by temptations to grave sin, of which hell is the punishment, as when we are considering those daily faults, of which hell is the image. But now, there are some people who find it very difficult to focus on eternity at all. The whole notion of it seems cloudy and unfamiliar; if they try to meditate on heaven—still more on hell—they lose all sense of reality about it; imagination fails them, and they have to fall back upon bare faith. Most of us are like that some of the time, and some of us are like that most of the time. What are we to do about it?

Why, if we feel like that, I think the best thing is to tell Almighty God that we know, and he knows, we are dreadfully inadequate receiving instruments for supernatural truth. Our minds are earth-bound, our consciences are not sensitive enough to bridge the gulf between heaven and hell. *Our* idea of heaven, then, shall be the vision of God after death, in which we shall see clearly all that is now dark to us. And we shall fear, after death, an eternity in which our present craving for light will remain for ever unsatisfied; in which we shall know our guilt, but shall not repent of it, acknowledge the justice of our sentence, but not be reconciled to it. Eternity without God is hell; eternity with God is heaven; enough is said, if we know so much as that about eternity.

19 But Only Christ

I WOULD just like to finish this retreat by giving you a single thought, in the hope that it will sometimes recur to your mind and sum up what I have been trying to say to you. The thought I would like you to carry away is a text from the story of the Transfiguration, "Immediately looking about them, they saw no man any more, but Jesus only with them."

Our Lord used to go up into a mountain when he wanted to pray; and such retirement is a fitting parable of the aim we set before ourselves when we go into retreat. We go up into a mountain so as to be alone, so as to get away from the press of business and from the daily companionships which distract our minds from God. We want to leave behind us, for a little, those enervating airs of the valley— our daily habits of sloth and self-indulgence which enfeeble our spiritual system. We want to be in a position to take, for once, a bird's eye view of our whole spiritual situation; to see the past, the present and the future mapped out for us by distance, as we cannot see them when we are about our daily work, because the claims of the moment are too insistent with us.

And it is a mountain of transfiguration. In so far as we

succeed in making a good retreat, we succeed in setting
before ourselves, in a clearer light than before, the Figure of
the Master whom we serve. We see, in a stronger contrast
of light and shadow, how much he has done for us and how
little we have done for him; what a claim he makes on our
lives and how little we have done to satisfy that claim. Even
in a retreat made carelessly and perfunctorily, we shall have
been given some lights which made us see a little more
clearly his unique majesty, and his love for us, and our ingratitude to him.

There appeared, on the mountain of Transfiguration,
two other figures together with our Lord, Moses and Elias.
Perhaps you are beginning to feel by now that you have
heard enough about the Old Testament. But there is no
need to look for deep or far-fetched symbolism here; there
is no doubt that Moses and Elias represent the Law and the
Prophets. And you, too, in your retreat, trying to look, as
well as your dazzled eyes would let you, at the glorious figure of our Lord Jesus Christ, became conscious also of the
defects in your own life. You came to see more clearly that
here and here your life transgresses, or is in danger of trans-
gressing, the spirit of that moral law which God has laid
down for our observance. And your conscience was enlightened, to see more clearly what such disobedience on
your part meant, its possible consequences in time and in
eternity. The Law to direct you, prophecy to kindle your
affections, these, too, have had a place in your retreat.

"Lord," says St. Peter, speaking at random amid the
splendours of the vision, "Lord, it is good for us to be here;
let us build three tabernacles." He wishes that the experience could go on for ever. And some of us, I hope, will have

felt at one point or another during this retreat that an or-
dered life of prayer and meditation was a thing to be desired,
if only our state of life allowed it, as a permanent thing;
that it was more natural, more acceptable to our higher
natures, than the rough-and-tumble of life. Well, that is
not to be; we have to come down from the mountain, and
find ourselves in close touch with the thronging multitudes
again. The world will be at our elbow, and the lessons we
learned on the mountain-top will efface themselves all too
readily.

I can offer you no better counsel, I can wish you no more
appropriate grace, than what is contained in these words
which describe the coming down of the apostles from the
mountain of Transfiguration; "immediately looking about
them they saw no man any more, but Jesus only with them."
They saw no man any more—not Moses, even, with those
tablets of the Law which he received, engraved by divine
fingers, on the Mount of Sinai; not Elias, even, in the rugged
grandeur of his inspiration. I should not wish you to leave
this retreat nervously or scrupulously alarmed about the
state of your soul; wondering whether your confessions in
the past have been good confessions, whether there is any
chance that you, in your weakness, will be able to avoid
future occasions of sin. I should not wish you to be over-
whelmed with terror at the thought of the judgements
which await impenitent sinners. No, "Jesus only with
them"; better that you should go away with the sense of a
Divine Friend, always at your side to check, to console, to
encourage you; a Friend whose presence you make your
own whenever you will turn to him, amidst the press of
secular occupations, in a devout moment of recollection.

No man any more, but Jesus only—yes, you will meet the people you are accustomed to meet; but if only you would learn in meeting them to see Jesus in them! Is there some face that tempts you with memories of unholy desires in the past? You will see behind it a soul which Jesus loves, a soul in which Jesus desires to express his own image. Is there someone who has done you injury, who provokes you to anger? Is there someone whose conversation bores you, whose importunity wearies you, whose outward manners offend you? Here too you will see Jesus only—the Crucified appealing to you out of those human souls, that need your care, your forbearance, your compassion. Jesus with you, not an abstract idea, not a historical memory, not enthroned in the terrors of Judgement, but a Friend, human and divine, constantly at your side, sharing your burdens, understanding your difficulties, sympathizing with your work.

Let us pray for one another that we may at all times learn and do God's Holy Will. As I bring this retreat to an end, I will not ask pardon for what I have said or what I have left unsaid; God uses our words as he will, and he can bring good out of any retreat, whoever the preacher. For the same reason, I will not seek to engage your gratitude if, here and there, the right word has been said or the right impulse given; it is in God's hands. Only I would ask for your prayers, I who have said all this to you when I needed so much more to have said it to me; your charitable prayers, lest perhaps when I have preached to others I myself should become a castaway.